indéscrete
indivisitive
indented
ged upon
inaudibl
interrogative
INSTINCTIVE
instant-access
inward
improvised if only
incapac
inter-tw
INCUBATO
inappropriate
interpersonal
INEXACT
indistinct
ICBM
interrupted
impoverished
mpatient
insulated
immune
invented
independent
indomitable irksome
institutionalized
INCONSPICUOUS
irre
sible
tent INCONCLUSIVE
import-export
inspired
illicit
in-store promotio
insat
terlude
INVADER
irresistible
improved
IMPERILL
INFAM
intuit
BALANCED
informed
ideological
indoors
interdependent
incisive
mpeded
interviewed
nextricable
Indecisive
interested
informal
Interspe
irate
in situ
indebted
inattentive
inward-
ERWOVEN
ILLEGAL
fluenza
irrevocable
instructional
infrared
indenture
ee
in-flight
defensible IDIOTIC
intern implored interes
irrational
IMPLODED
intercepted
indecent
innovative
incessant
indefatigable
introverted
impressionable
duced
isolationist
isolated
increasing
illatease
introspective
indulgent
ill insecure
invulnerable
indelicate
ecise interior design
invaluable
inner circle
implied
IGNORED
instrumental
ICK indelible
impractic
innocent
intercourse
influx interdenominational
used IMPOUNDED
interpolated
incidental
INADMISSIBLE
infame IMPRESSIONABLE
irreverent
INACTIVE
ineligible
irresponsible
itemized
impulse buyer
inorganic
inoperable
issue-oriented
individualistic
ingenious
incalculable
IMAGE
interracial
Insulted
IMPROVED
VORY TOWER
inventive
indoctrinated
inebriated
incandescent
industrious
in-flight
ner-city
innumerable
interchangeable
inbox
imeressionable
immediate
ILLUMINATED
inching
ill-fated
INADVERTENT

WITHDRAWN

361817

306.46
LOG

13.23
us
9/06
z

PRAISE for MY FIRST BOOK
(If We Ever Break Up, This Is My Book)

"Sly cartoons that manage to be funny
about the fragility of love."
—*New York Magazine*

"Poignant illustrations and captions about
the universal but lonely truths of breaking up."
—*Maclean's*

"Funny and helpful."
—*USA Today*

"Anchoring the unmoored in the choppy
waters of bewilderment."
—*Nashville City Paper*

ST. ALBERT PUBLIC LIBRARY
5 ST. ANNE STREET
ST. ALBERT, ALBERTA T8N 3Z9

ABOUT THE AUTHOR

JASON LOGAN is a freelance illustrator who has done work for *The New York Times* and *Maclean's*. He is the author and illustrator of *If We Ever Break Up, This Is My Book*. Logan lives in Toronto.

iGeneration

SHUFFLING TOWARD THE FUTURE

Jason Logan

VIKING
CANADA

VIKING CANADA

Published by the Penguin Group

Penguin Group (Canada), 90 Eglinton Avenue East, Suite 700, Toronto, Ontario, Canada M4P 2Y3
(a division of Pearson Canada Inc.)

Penguin Group (USA) Inc., 375 Hudson Street, New York, New York 10014, U.S.A.
Penguin Books Ltd, 80 Strand, London WC2R 0RL, England
Penguin Ireland, 25 St Stephen's Green, Dublin 2, Ireland (a division of Penguin Books Ltd)
Penguin Group (Australia), 250 Camberwell Road, Camberwell, Victoria 3124, Australia
(a division of Pearson Australia Group Pty Ltd)
Penguin Books India Pvt Ltd, 11 Community Centre, Panchsheel Park, New Delhi – 110 017, India
Penguin Group (NZ), cnr Airborne and Rosedale Roads, Albany, Auckland 1310, New Zealand
(a division of Pearson New Zealand Ltd)
Penguin Books (South Africa) (Pty) Ltd, 24 Sturdee Avenue, Rosebank, Johannesburg 2196,
South Africa

Penguin Books Ltd, Registered Offices: 80 Strand, London WC2R 0RL, England

First published 2006

(RRD)   10 9 8 7 6 5 4 3 2 1

Copyright © Jason Logan, 2006

All rights reserved. Without limiting the rights under copyright reserved above, no part of this
publication may be reproduced, stored in or introduced into a retrieval system, or transmitted in
any form or by any means (electronic, mechanical, photocopying, recording or otherwise), without
the prior written permission of both the copyright owner and the above publisher of this book.

iPod, iTunes, iLife, and QuickTime are trademarks of Apple Computer, Inc., registered in the
U.S. and other countries. *iGeneration* is an independent publication of Penguin Group (Canada)
and has not been authorized, sponsored, or otherwise approved by Apple Computer, Inc.

The following are also registered trademarks of their respective owners: Amazon, American Apparel,
Answers.com, Ask Jeeves, Beanie Babies, Bentley, BlackBerry, Cabbage Patch Kids, Disneyland,
eBay, Everything2, Flikr, Frisbee, Google, GORE-TEX, Kinkos, LEGO, Lululemon, MapQuest,
Mediabistro, Monster.com, MSN, Myspace.com, Netflix, PayPal, PalmPilot, Photoshop, Q-tips,
Rubik's Cube, Slashdot, Starbucks, Tater Tots, Yahoo. All other products or services may be
trademarks or registered trademarks of their respective owners.

*Publisher's note: This book is a work of fiction. Names, characters, places and incidents
either are the product of the author's imagination or are used fictitiously, and any
resemblance to actual persons living or dead, events, or locales is entirely coincidental.*

Manufactured in the U.S.A.

ISBN-10: 0-670-06607-9
ISBN-13: 978-0-670-06607-0

Library and Archives Canada Cataloguing in Publication data available upon request

Visit the Penguin Group (Canada) website at **www.penguin.ca**

Special and corporate bulk purchase rates available; please see
www.penguin.ca/corporatesales or call 1-800-399-6858, ext. 477 or 474

DEDICATION

FOR THE BUG

<u>AUTHOR'S NOTE:</u>

EVERYTHING IS OUT
OF DATE THESE DAYS

It often happens that I wake up at night and begin to think about a serious problem and decide I must tell the Pope about it. Then I wake up completely and remember that I am the Pope!

—Pope John XXIII

DON'T TOUCH THAT DIAL

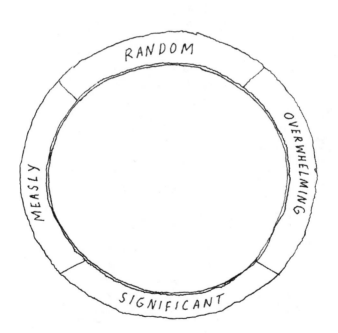

WORST-CASE SCENARIO

YOUR FRIEND WILL CRASH AT YOUR APARTMENT FOR A COUPLE OF WEEKS

HIS OVERUSE OF YOUR iPod WILL CAUSE IT TO CRASH YOUR COMPUTER

THIS WILL CAUSE YOUR SERVER TO CRASH, WHICH IN TURN WILL CAUSE SOME BIGGER SERVER TO CRASH

WHICH WILL OF COURSE CAUSE THE NETWORK TO CRASH WHICH WILL CAUSE THE BIG NETWORK TO CRASH WHICH WILL CAUSE THE PLANE TO CRASH WHICH WILL CAUSE THAT MOVIE _CRASH_ TO PLUMMET IN FOREIGN DVD SALES WHICH (NOW THAT I THINK ABOUT IT) WOULDN'T REALLY BE THE END OF THE WORLD...

FEEL LIKE YOU ARE IN A FREEFALL?

ACTUALLY, EVERYTHING IS.

A LIST OF
NEW THINGS THAT
SOUND LIKE OTHER THINGS
and THAT PUT TOGETHER MIGHT MAKE
THE START OF A KIND OF WEIRD
Children's Story

- COOKIES
- MONSTER
- MOUSE
- APPLE

PRIDE COMES BEFORE A CRASH

⮡ Yes I _did_ mistakenly try to download a Russian bride.

⮡ My eyes _were_ bigger than my hard drive.

⮡ I _do_ have about 17 programs going right now.

⮡ I suppose I _did_ try to wire up my iPod to write that essay for me.

⮡ And yes, my cat _was_ entrusted with the task of replacing the batteries.

⮡ over and out

I'd say you deserve whatever you get, and have you noticed how fluffy my fur is?

101 THINGS TO DO WITH YOUR DEAD iPod

(OK 50)

1. Compose an e-sonnet to it
2. Use it as some sort of neo-throwing star
3. Harvest the bits of gold from its chip
4. Use it as a fairly heavy stickie note
5. Create earbud jewellery out of it
6. Make into a coffee warmer for mom
7. Try to sell it to someone on craigslist
8. Keep it until it can be valued on <u>Antiques Roadshow</u>
9. It's not dead, it's sleeping
10. Melt down, refashion into hood ornament
11. Skip it on a lake
12. Put it on the wall of your isolated cabin with the other taxidermied gadgets
13. Just buy another one
14. Take to dump, explore dump
15. Buy another one and put all parts of new one into the old one
16. Pretend this isn't happening. Go into a period of denial
17. Use it to smash all those other devices that are annoying you
18. Put it beside that Rubik's Cube
19. Cut it up and try to piece it together with your Lego
20. Scan it for god-knows-what purpose
21. Send it back to the manufacturer along with your manifesto on planned obsolescences
22. Use it as a reference to the colour white
23. Use it as a doorstop
24. Use it as a very small speed bump
25. Could use it as a skateboard brake

26. Burn it to keep warm on a cold winter's night

27. Burn it to get high on the fumes

28. Quarantine it to protect your other devices

29. Use it as a sort of stand for your gun

30. Use it as a sort of stand for your cactus

31. Add to plate rail

32. Try really shining it up for use as a mirror

33. Use it to pick up after your pet

34. Imagine that it is a stage for tiny rockstars

35. Place it in breast pocket: this may save you from a mob hit

36. You never used it anyway

37. Recycle

38. Lipstick tester?

39. Credit card demagnetizer?

40. Hat for small robot?

41. Put it down your pants to impress the ladies with... no, wait, it's not quite the right shape

42. Use it as an erasable x's and o's board

43. Use it as a non-returning boomerang

44. Replace that tile in the bathroom with it

45. Makes an elegant sashimi tray

46. Keep wearing it, it still works as a conversation stopper

47. Use it to confirm small weight measurements, like for example that piece of hash you just overpaid for

48. Use this experience to begin to think about your own death

49. Check it for fingerprints

50. How about some sort of funeral?

iFuneral

At least we still have each other.
He's shuffled off this mortal coil...
that's right, bud.
I always said he was a little too thin.
I guess this means there'll be no music.

WHEN THE DUST FINALLY SETTLES

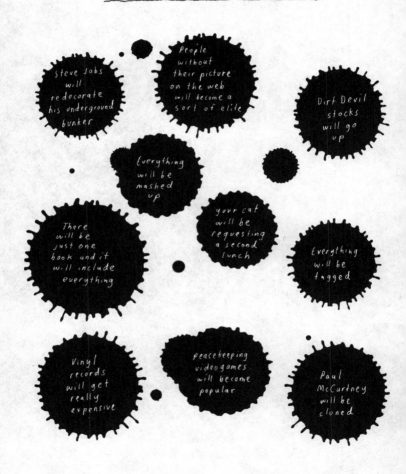

ARE YOU PREPARED?

PURE
SPRING
CARBON-
FILTERED
RARE
GLACIAL-
HARVESTED
WATER

WHY YOU LEFT ON FOOT

Because my car broke down. OK, so it was my parents' minivan. The point is, I think vehicles are evil. And, I've been trying to get rid of some of the dead weight in my life. You know— go totally unplugged. Plus, all my batteries seemed to have died at the same time. And anyway, google images was seeming less and less like exploring, and I was also reading about flâneur culture, and I bought these new shoes and...

WHY YOU CAME BACK

turns out the real is scarier than the virtual

LOOKING FOR HOME —

which one of these work for you?

HOME PLATE
gives you a good
feeling if you slide
in before anyone
catches you.

*you sure
are home
late — and
what's that
funny smell?*

YOUR PARENTS' HOME
gives you a good feeling
if you slide in before
anyone realizes that you
are wasted.

RUBY SLIPPERS
Get you home. Although
I sure as hell wouldn't
try to walk to Kansas in them.

NAUTILUS
its construction
has something to
do with some guy
called Fibonacci, I think.
Looks fairly sturdy
anyway.

COMPUTER VERSION OF HOME
is actually kind of
comforting when you
are far away.

APOCALYPSE

_or_

JUST A VERY

IMPRESSIVE SUNSET

< you make the call >

TO: the God of small, medium-sized, and big things
RE: PRAYER
CC: < other available gods >   BCC: Steve Jobs

"LET THERE BE LIGHT"

      and let that light not be the greenish
      glow of the fluorescent tubing at my job,
      nor let that light be the cancerously
      bright sun angered by our dismissive relationship
      to the atmosphere. Nor, indeed, let it be the
      periwinkle glow from my laptop (which
      has begun to give me headaches).

      Yeah, instead let it be the orangey glow
      from a candle in some hip bar in the
      hip section of a hip city. You know, the
      sort of flickering light that makes my skin
      look good. And while you are at it,
      perhaps you could throw in a date for me :)

AM I BEING PLAGUED BY A WRATHFUL GOD*?

Let's have a look at my trials

* ANGERED PERHAPS BY MY OVERUSE/ UNDERUSE OF TECHNOLOGY

the TRIALS of INFORMATION

The TRIAL of WATER

the TRIAL of ENDURANCE

one of these doesn't work, although, I just bought them all

the TRIAL of SUSTENANCE

the TRIAL of the COUCH

← Technologically advanced but nothing in there (except for this here carrot)

the TRIAL of the PLANTS

↳ even the cactus has seen better days

SHALL WE COMPARE?

Complex,
patterned,
repetitive,
and ultimately
kind of
lonely

Same here

ACTING NATURAL

(Some Do's and Don'ts)

DO

☐ Get some fresh air every once in a while

☐ Try a non-frozen dinner from time to time

☐ Dance in the dark (be careful)

☐ Try a non-video game or two

☐ Frolic in rainstorms (be very careful)

DON'T

☐ Make a special website devoted to documenting, and commenting on, pictures of yourself

☐ Try to base your emotions on emoticons

☐ Overbrush your hair

☐ Get too obsessed with those self-help websites

☐ Do too much copying and pasting in your emails

KEY

① *TREE* I believe that the cinnamon from my lattes and the corks from my wine come from this

② *SEASONS* This is what they call change in the country

③ BROKEN-DOWN OLD FENCE: Note to self: may fetch quite a high price on eBay

④ SEAGULLS, I THINK Probably heading back to the city where the living is easier

⑤ *OLD GREY BARN* Looks kind of like a loft on the inside

⑥ *THE AIR* No sign of Wifi. Dial-up connection at best

⑦ ANIMALS A category which seems to include mostly bugs

⑧ *TALL GRASS WAVING IN THE WIND* May contain the remains of Jimmy Hoffa

⑨ *THE ROAD TO NOWHERE* We have these in the city, too

⑥

⑦ ←

They were really reminding me
of the new iLife package

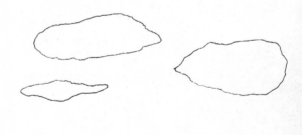

They're just clouds

BACK IN THE CITY

the sky

The smog

the skyline

the graffiti

the sidewalk

the smell of pee

(which, admittedly, I _am_
partially responsible for)

DOING A LOT OF SURFING?

DON'T FORGET TO MIND THE
STINGING JELLYFISH

HOW WELL DO YOU KNOW the MODERN WORLD
of SIGNS and SYMBOLS?

NAME	SYMBOL	EXPLANATION
YOKE ?		- what the heck does it mean? - Couldn't find anything on the Lululemon site - Interesting though, turned on its side, →ⱺ looks a lot like Hobo sign that means "This owner is out" www.slackaction.com/signroll.htm - very weird
WOMAN SYMBOL		Really took off in the 60s and 70s when all those gains were made for women
MAN SYMBOL		worn on a chain at chest-level will, if anything, make you less of a man
ANKH		Important to the Kabbalah, and vampires too, and incidently looks suspiciously like the form of Kenny from South Park, but you would know this if you'd been spending as much time as I have on the net
ALIEN/ PAIR OF UNDERWEAR ?		you make the call

LAST NIGHT

SURFED MYSELF
TO SLEEP

THIS MORNING

AWOKE WITH
THE GREAT DREAD

CHARTING THE UNKNOWN

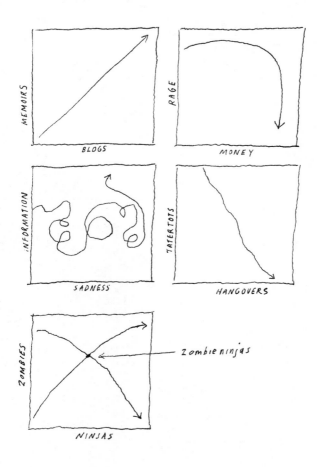

Man is still the most extraordinary computer of all.

—John Fitzgerald Kennedy

Is there more nothing than something or more something than nothing?

THE CONSTANTLY CHANGING SELF

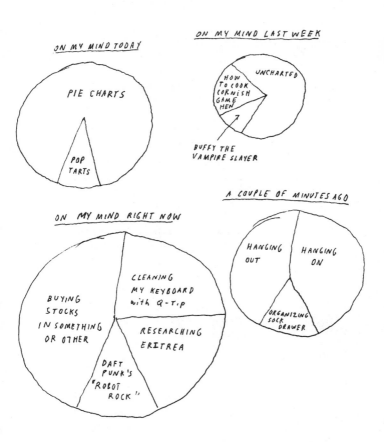

ON MY MIND TODAY

PIE CHARTS

POP TARTS

ON MY MIND LAST WEEK

UNCHARTED

HOW TO COOK CORNISH GAME HEN

BUFFY THE VAMPIRE SLAYER

A COUPLE OF MINUTES AGO

HANGING OUT

HANGING ON

ORGANIZING SOCK DRAWER

ON MY MIND RIGHT NOW

BUYING STOCKS IN SOMETHING OR OTHER

CLEANING MY KEYBOARD with Q-TIP

RESEARCHING ERITREA

DAFT PUNK'S "ROBOT ROCK"

How soon do you have to deal with that message? Let's check:

THE EMAIL TRIAGE

RED ALERT
(right away)

family emergencies (that appear to involve a will)

friends breaking up (and particularly those whose partner you've always been kind of interested in)

AMBER
(soon)

work stuff (and only those messages that help you make enough money to maintain your slacker lifestyle)

SPAM, but really good spam, like for instance there's some pretty amazing pills out there on the net

YELLOW
(soonish)

forwarded QuickTime movies involving last night (which to you is pretty much all black)

WHAT-EV'S
(whenever)

sure it's marked important, but hey, if they really need to get ahold of you they can text your friends

GETTING TO KNOW YOUR COMPUTER KEYPAD

KEY	FUNCTION	WHAT IT SHOULD DO
⏎	Gets you to the next line.	Get you to move out of your parents' basement.
CTRL	I think helps with those illusive Spanish accents.	Actually help you to control something in your life. OR Help with control issues.
DEL	Gets rid of character or line.	Should delete all kinds of unwanted things.
ENTER	Gets you to the next line.	Garden of Eden?
ALT	Use with other keys to make stuff happen.	Give you some sense of what's going on in the world of alternative music.
HOME	Returns you to the beginning.	Help with parents somehow.
ESC	Supposed to help when computer is frozen, but this never worked for me.	Get you somewhere nice. Like, say, Aruba.
⬭	space.	Help deal with your increasing number of roommates.

TODAY:

everything is connected but nothing is
really illuminated

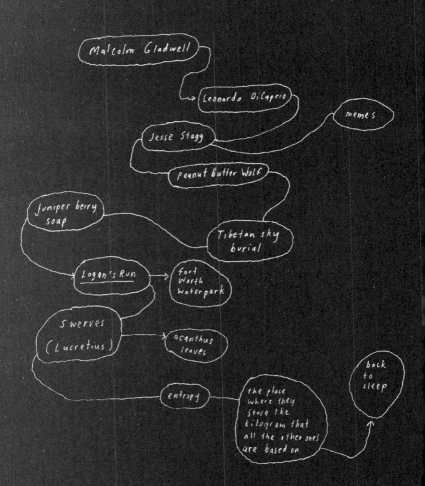

BEYOND GOOGLE'S POWER TO EXPLAIN

> How exactly mini-muffins are made

> OK, but why?

> AND WHY do I have this continuing
attachment to "QUACKERS", the
stuffed animal duck, a relationship
that admittedly may predate the internet?

> HOW do the Canadians manage to
produce so many pop divas

> OK , BUT WHY?

Q and As

~ some superficial questions finally answered ~

Q. WILL THE COMPUTER SCREEN MAKE MY SKIN
LOOK OLD?

A. Eventually, yes.

Q. WILL THERE COME A TIME WHEN VIRTUAL
REALITY WILL MAKE IT NOT MATTER WHAT
I LOOK LIKE?

A. No, never.

Q. WILL THE IRISH CONTINUE TO CORNER THE
PUB-DECORATION MARKET?

A. Yep, as technologically advanced as they are,
the Irish just can't help exporting cardboard
celtic harps and leprechauns.

Q. WILL GUM GET LESS, OR MORE, "INTENSE"?

A. It will toggle, but I did notice an attempt
to brand "less intense" gum at my corner store.

Q. WILL IT BE POSSIBLE FOR SECRETARIES
TO ORDER ROUNDS OF SAMBUCA SHOOTERS ONLINE?

A. Oh, that's probably already happening, but the
word secretary is sounding really out of date.

and a few more.

Q. CARROTS? ANY CHANGES?

A. Bigger, oranger, and will taste something like celery.

Q. WILL CAR ADS CONTINUE TO CLAIM THAT THERE IS AN OPEN ROAD?

A. Oh yes, even more so.

Q. WHEN DO YOU GET OFF WORK?

A. You know, I'm not sure that I'll ever get off work.

WHAT YOUR ICONS ARE REALLY SAYING

SADNESS AMONG YOUR GADGETS

IS IT TIME TO MONITOR YOUR PARENTS' INTERNET USE?

YOUR MUSIC — REMIXED

WHAT THE HELL AM I SUPPOSED
TO DO WHILST MY MUSIC IS DOWNLOADING?

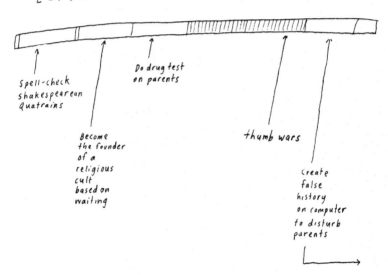

[2% COMPLETE : TIME REMAINING APPROXIMATELY 7 HOURS 22.5 MINUTES]

Spell-check
shakespearean
quatrains

Become
the founder
of a
religious
cult
based on
waiting

Do drug test
on parents

thumb wars

Create
false
history
on computer
to disturb
parents

A SAMPLE FALSE HISTORY
TO DISTURB YOUR PARENTS WITH

HISTORY CACHE

www. panda-child-acid .xxx
http://www. makeabomboutofcommonhouseholdproducts.com
www. freeoldmansex.nz.org
www. prisons + welfare + lifeplan .com
+ make _ some _ cash _ while _ in _ prison. com

* QUIZ FOR PARENTS *

HOW OUT OF TOUCH R U ?

MAPQUEST IS: A) SOME SORT OF *Da Vinci Code* SPINOFF

B) A PIRATE-FINDING DEVICE

C) THE WAY I GET TO MY DRUG DEALER'S HOUSE

D) LOADED INTO MY DOG'S GPS FEED

Your Parents' Useless Crystal

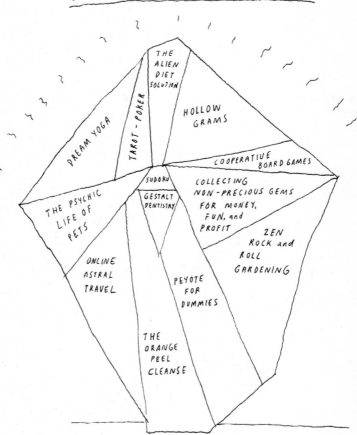

WHAT IS IT WITH COFFEE and NEW TECHNOLOGY?
Let's compare, shall we?

COFFEE

Hot

Sort of exotic

increasingly
overpriced

At first it
makes you
feel excited and
then you feel
sort of ill
and disoriented
if you have
too much

NEW TECHNOLOGY

Hot

sort of exotic

increasingly
overpriced

Full of
stupid
comparisons
like this

☐ DOUBLE

☐ EXTRA SHOT

☐ MAYBE
YOU SHOULD
JUST BE
GETTING
MORE
SLEEP

LAST RESORTS FOR INFORMATION

☐ SUMERIAN CLAY TABLETS

☐ DEWEY DECIMAL SYSTEM

☐ WIKIPEDIA

☐ ASK JEEVES

☐ EVERYTHING2.COM

☐ YOUR DAD

TRASH IT

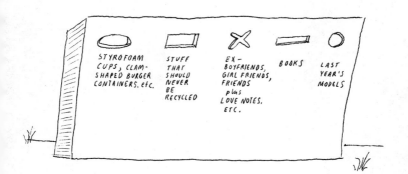

STYROFOAM
CUPS, CLAM-
SHAPED BURGER
CONTAINERS, etc.

STUFF
THAT
SHOULD
NEVER
BE
RECYCLED

EX-
BOYFRIENDS,
GIRL FRIENDS,
FRIENDS
plus
LOVE NOTES,
ETC.

BOOKS

LAST
YEAR'S
MODELS

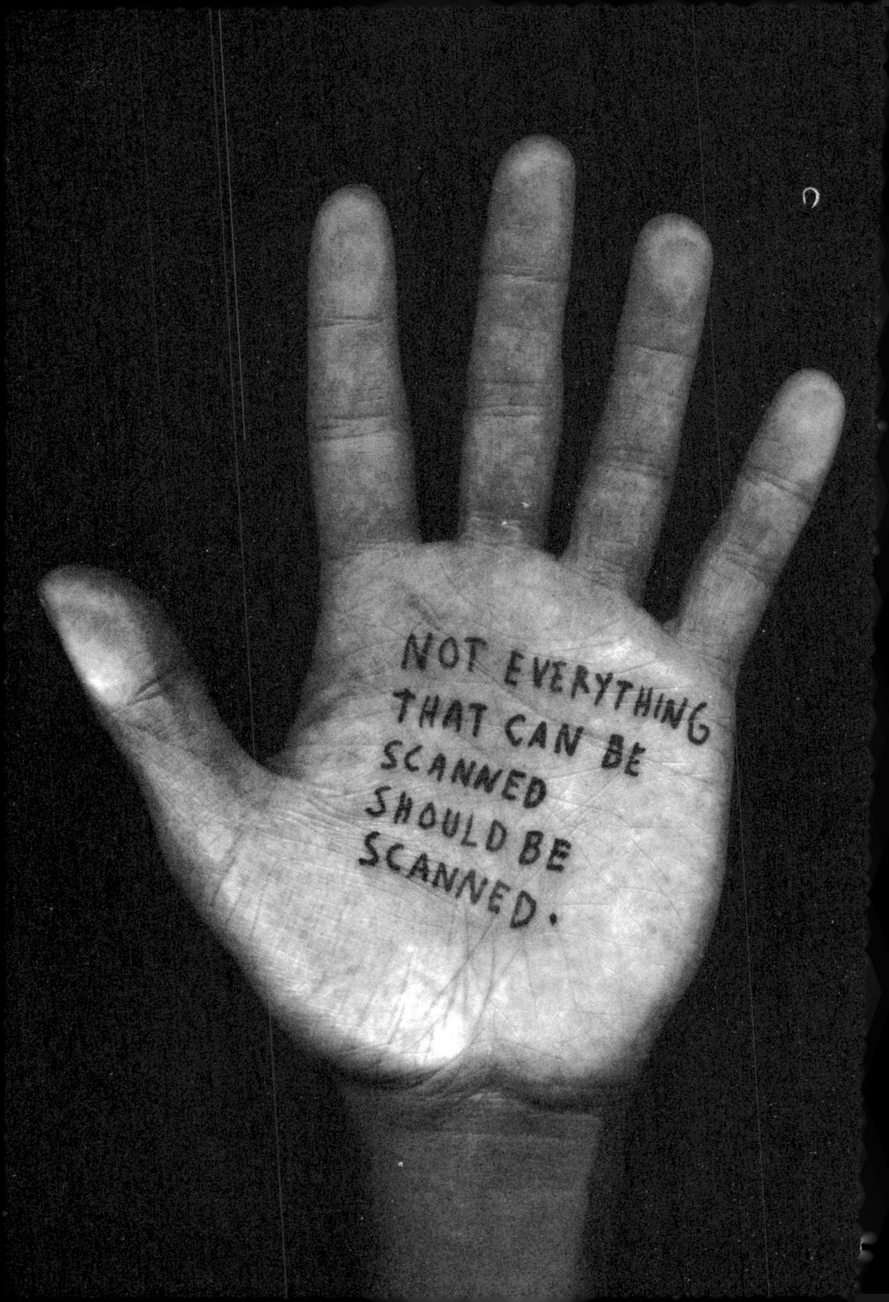
NOT EVERYTHING
THAT CAN BE
SCANNED
SHOULD BE
SCANNED.

Figures are meaningless in the context of people's concrete experiences.

—Nelson Mandela

DO YOU HAVE ENOUGH ENERGY FOR THE ENERGETIC NEW FUTURE?

➤ Rate yourself on this handy scale ⟵

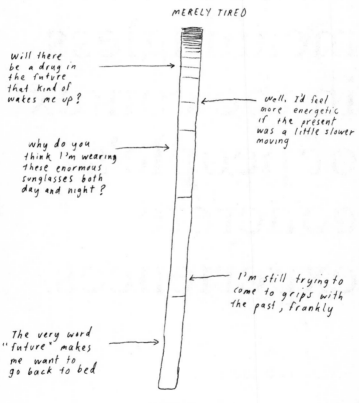

MERELY TIRED

Will there be a drug in the future that kind of wakes me up?

Well, I'd feel more energetic if the present was a little slower moving

why do you think I'm wearing these enormous sunglasses both day and night?

I'm still trying to come to grips with the past, frankly

The very word "future" makes me want to go back to bed

COMPLETELY EXHAUSTED

THE HAND

Long considered merely an extension of the arm, the HAND is finally starting to be recognized as a high-tech gadget

LET'S HAVE A CLOSER LOOK AT ITS COMPONENTS:

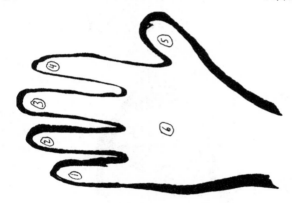

① __THE BABY__ good for hitting that hard-to-reach "z" key—
Do not leave unattended

② __THE RING FINGER__ has nothing to do with ringtones,
I think this one is mostly decorative

③ __THE MIDDLE FINGER__ useful as a primitive go away signal

④ __POINTER__ good with on/off button. not bad with iPod dial,
too

⑤ __THUMB__ for texting + getting rides

⑥ __PALM__ not affiliated in any way with the Palm Pilot.
OK, maybe a little bit

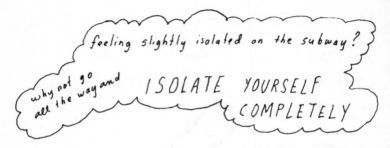

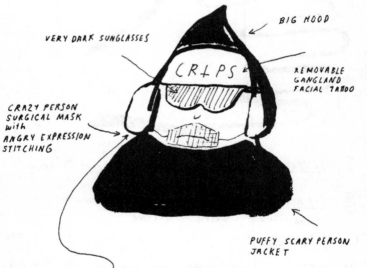

Welcome to the Modern Paradox

0%

After consuming 4 energy bars, 2 xtra Ginkgopower drinks, 1 higher life protein shake, 3 wake-up pills, 1 double energizer shot of wheatgrass, and after powering up and recharging my iPod, BlackBerry, and high-speed, Wifi-equipped laptop, I feel completely exhausted.

9 PM , Tuesday   (low tech)

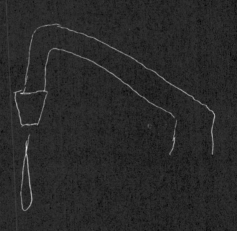

FIGURE I'LL JUST STAY HOME
TONIGHT

WHAT SORT OF BRAIN DO YOU HAVE?

and what can it do for you?

the SMALL Brain

the MEDIUM Brain

the LARGE Brain

(ADVANTAGES)	(DISADVANTAGES)	+	−	+	−
They don't call me a "happy little idiot" for nothing	sometimes bump into things	can understand the lyrics to most songs	Can't understand the melody when trying to sing along (unfortunately)	Ability to process huge amounts of the Information Age	Most of that information is totally useless
not much for the alcohol to destroy	OK, quite often bump into things, but I forget about it almost immediately	can fit in with lots of people, especially "regular" people	those "regular people" aren't exactly challenging me	Good at worldly chit chat at parties	overly aware of the world's troubles
				feeling of superiority	feeling of isolation
					plus, sometimes hard to hold head up

6 new diseases that you may not be aware of yet

① CHRONICAL FATIGUE SYNDROME

More!

Lord of the Rings, Narnia, Harry Potter — I can't take this anymore

② UNSEASONAL AFFECTIVE DISORDER

Even really warm temperatures in the winter don't seem to cheer you up — if anything they just make you nervous about the polar ice caps

* see also BIPOLAR DEPRESSION

③ HYPOMANIA

often affects businesspeople and LA-types. Goes undiagnosed because they like being so busy

④ HYPER AWARENESS OF AUTISM DISORDER

Look, Honey, it says RIGHT HERE that our child may be getting autism from cereal!

⑤ ACQUIRED SITUATIONAL NARCISCISM

see Robert Hillman's Cornell study. Note Michael Jackson, Russel Crowe, etc, people who feel that the world revolves around them because it kind of does. Still kind of a sickness though.

Hey, it's not my fault

⑥ UNDIAGNOSED PERSONAL FINANCIAL DEPRESSION

I'm sure it'll be fine

wait'll she sees my Paypal expenses

THINGS I'VE FORGOTTEN

meaningful dreams

how to use paragraphs

what real file folders
look like

my cat's mother's maiden
name (which incidentally is
also my password for online banking)

what strawberries are supposed
to taste like

the difference between a condo,
a loft, and just a small apartment
that is really expensive

the difference between a hard drive,
userspace, home, and a desktop. All
of which could use a little tidying up.

WHAT HAVE YOU GOTTEN INTO BED WITH

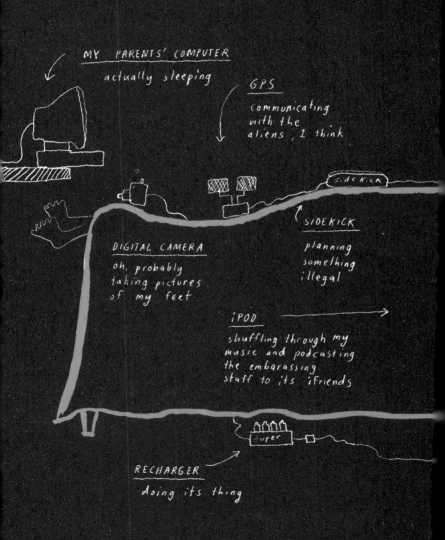

MY PARENTS' COMPUTER
actually sleeping

GPS
communicating
with the
aliens, I think

SIDEKICK

SIDEKICK
planning
something
illegal

DIGITAL CAMERA
oh, probably
taking pictures
of my feet

iPOD
shuffling through my
music and podcasting
the embarassing
stuff to its iFriends

super

RECHARGER
doing its thing

PARANOID, WEARY, OR GULLIBLE?

FRANKLY, I FIND THE REALITY OF 50,000 SONGS AT MY FINGERTIPS KIND OF FRIGHTENING.

THOSE DARK SILHOUETTES OF PEOPLE LISTENING TO MUSIC ARE MY FRIENDS. WE DRINK TOGETHER.

KEEPING YOU IN A STATE OF NOT QUITE UNDERSTANDING IS ALL PART OF THEIR PLAN.

WHO'S ASKING THIS? ARE YOU ONE OF THE POD PEOPLE?

I'M SUBLIMINAL TEXT MESSAGING YOU RIGHT NOW.

I'D UNPLUG MY PHONE BUT IT DOESN'T SEEM TO HAVE A PLUG.

THE LEADER OF OUR CULT DOESN'T BELIEVE WE SHOULD LET OURSELVES BE CONTROLLED BY TECHNOLOGY.

I JUST TRY NOT TO THINK ABOUT IT.

AM I ON DRUGS?   ## WILL I BE OKAY?

MAYBE NOT   IFFY   MAYBE SO

[X] [ ] [ ]   I am writing a sequel for Zeppelin called "Escalator to Hell"

[ ] [X] [ ]   Street lights are starting to look like UFOs

[ ] [ ] [X]   I will be playing a fairly central role in the Burning Man festival this year

[ ] [ ] [X]   I _was_ wondering why that muffin was green

[ ] [ ] [X]   My next move will require rolling very slowly

[ ] [ ] [ ] X   I'm pretty sure my cat is a wizard

SOURCES of ENERGY

GOOD	QUESTIONABLE	BAD
Solar wind	nuclear power	(certain) pills I've tried
friends (real)	turnips, and other bitter roots	(some) family members
early Beach Boys records		apartments (most)
	that fake smoke they have in clubs	the laser light they have in clubs

GETTING HIGH

	the very high		the sugar high	caffeine high	the first person shooter game high
	DRUGS	GOOD OLD BOOZE			
SYMPTOMS:	may experience a connection to certain Hollywood stars	Bumping into things	A feeling that life is good, all things are in harmony	Lots of ideas or at least the feeling that you have lots of ideas just biding their time until you have that second espresso	not sure, but I think this is mostly for weirdos
FOLLOWED BY:	a bit of a dark period if I remember correctly, and I'm not sure that I do.	a bit of a grey period and then a "going sober" period and then a disturbing "high on life" period	a feeling that all things other than your stomach are in harmony	Something weird with my tongue	probably end up with a government job of some kind or another

THE HANGOVER CURE

THERE IS NO
HANGOVER CURE

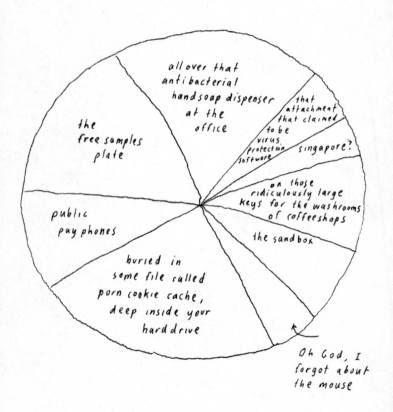

THE BUG

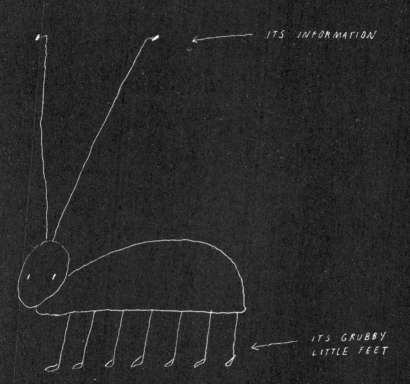

ITS INFORMATION

ITS GRUBBY
LITTLE FEET

TO WHAT EXTENT HAVE YOU FALSELY REPRESENTED YOURSELF ? *

- [ ] I <u>CAN</u> BLUFF MY WAY THROUGH ONLINE POKER
- [ ] WELL, I DRESS UP FOR HALLOWEEN
- [ ] OK, PRETTY MUCH EVERY DAY IS HALLOWEEN
- [ ] THE OCCASIONAL TRIP TO THE HAIRDRESSER
- [ ] PLATFORM SHOES
- [ ] DEGREES FROM SEVERAL PRESTIGIOUS ONLINE UNIVERSITIES
- [ ] A WHOLE VIRTUAL SELF THAT EVEN I DON'T FULLY UNDERSTAND
- [ ] WAS THIS A QUESTION FOR ME, OR MY CLONE?
- [ ] I FAILED THE CAPTCHA TEST

* more than a few checked boxes may point to a bit of a problem

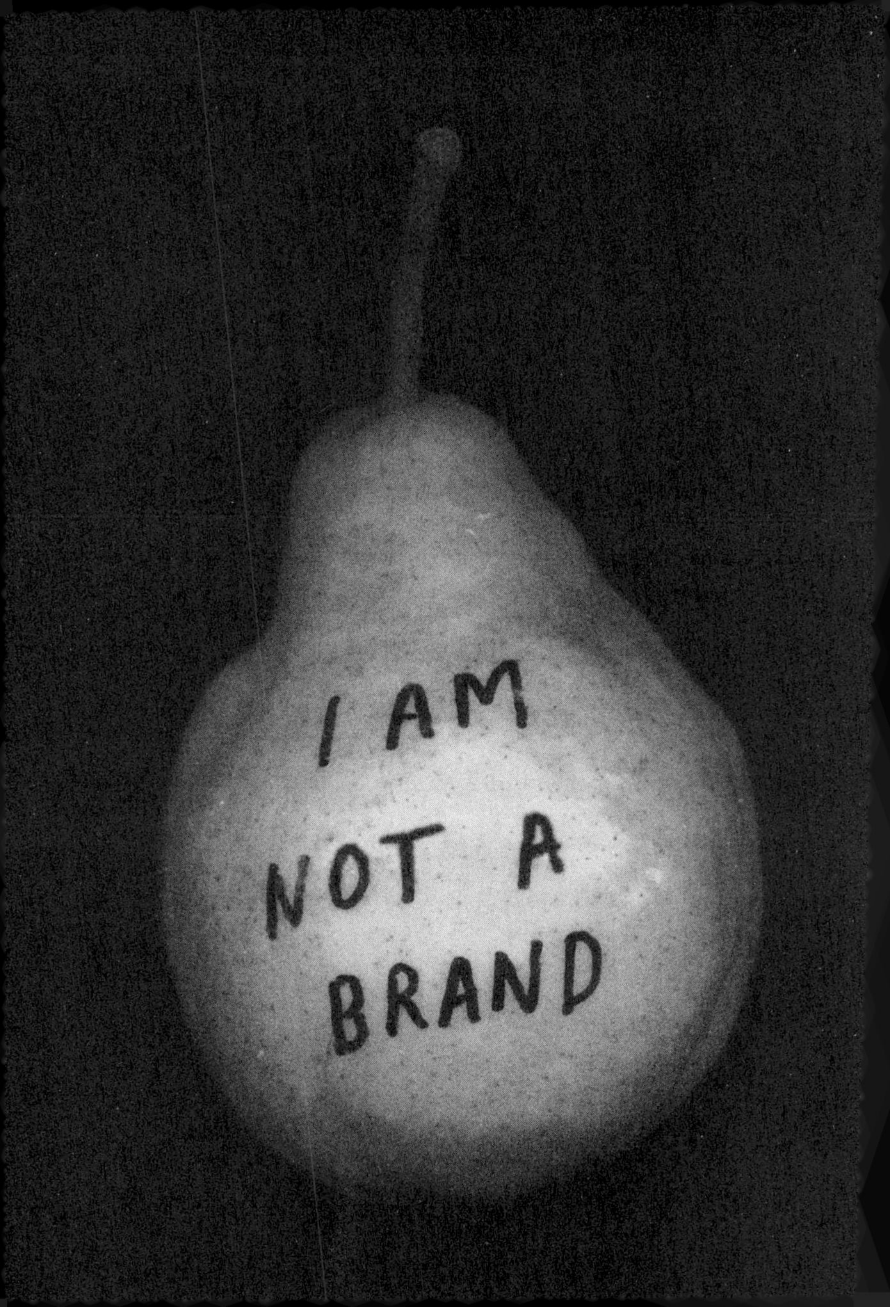
I AM
NOT A
BRAND

Must Not Sleep/Must Warn Others

—Tattoo on Aesop Rock's arm

comes in several sizes

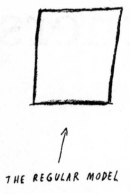

THE REGULAR MODEL

THE SUPERMODEL

WHERE DO I FIT IN?

THE SATELLITES

THE SKY

THE CULTURE

THE EARLY BIRD

THE MAINSTREAM

THE UNDERGROUND

A WORM

THE SUBCULTURE

THE SUB-SUBCULTURE

THE PEOPLE WHO SPEND
A LOT OF TIME IN BERLIN

THE ROOT OF ALL THINGS

ATTENTION ADVERTISERS

Trying to get a feel for this new youth market?

ADDING ANY OF THE FOLLOWING (AND PARTICULARLY IN COMBINATION) TO YOUR PRODUCT WILL GET YOU NOWHERE :

BUZZ
ULTIMATE
MEGA
PHAT
FRESH
SPA
EXTREME
BLING
ICE
CLEAR
MAX
JELLY
ZESTY !

AT THE CORE

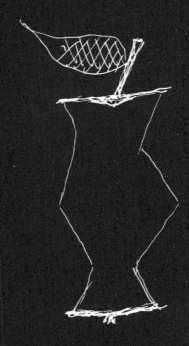

A BUNCH OF BITTER SEEDS

How things used to be
better in the olden days...

FOR CRIMINALS

HACKING

o very boring

o seems to involve
  quite a bit of
  math

o probably have to
  go to computer
  programming school

o end up eventually
  working for some
  bank or insurance
  company

HACK SAWING

o free bikes!

LISTMANIA

APPEARS
TO
BE
JUST
SOME
REGULAR
GUY'S
ATTEMPT
TO
PUT
TOGETHER
THE
RANDOM
SWEEPINGS
OF
STUFF
OUT
THERE
ON
THE
NET
BUT
IN
FACT
IT
IS
A
WELL-
THOUGHT-
OUT
SET
OF
WORDS
THAT
INEVITABLY
LEAD
TO
YOUR
INEXPLICABLY
BUYING
A
SECOND
COPY
OF
THE
DA VINCI CODE

thanks
O.B.

The Word is on the street

(OR AT LEAST ON THIS HERE WALL..

everything
has a
surface

The Candle
FLIKR'D
and
Went out

DON'T INFRINGE ON MY COPYRIGHT,
MAN

FACTS ARE BORING,
plus they're making
me a little sleepy

STOP the
TIME-AWARE
COSMOPOLITAN
ASSHOLES

HOW IN THE HELL
DO THEY DECAFFEINATE
COFFEE?

you're stepping
on my fantasy

iTunes
i don't get it

It may never really materialize for you, bub

FRESH FACE ON A DYING SCENE

Shoot the MSN Messenger

BE IN THE MOMENT FOR A MOMENT

SCRATCHED THE SURFACE,
I WON A DAY-OLD MINI-MUFFIN

NO TIME QUITE LIKE THE FUTURE

I WAS ALL THAT THEN BUT NOT NOW...

Pretty much everything is research

MORE IDEAS THAN CASH

HONEST SPAM

Balding, fat, impotant, broke, and
stupid? Please send us a ton of
cash and we'll send you nothing back.

Thanks,

The Management
(OK, just a bunch
of kids in their
parents' basement)

MAYBE the Eastern Europeans CAN HELP US HERE

(or at least provide us with a good metaphor...)

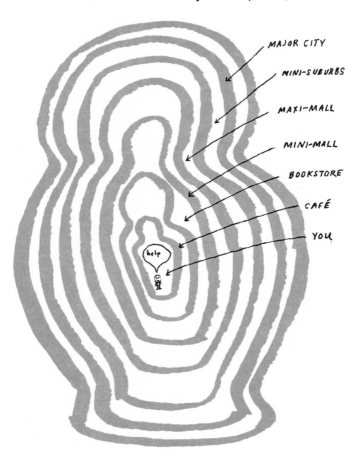

the FREE WORLD

FREE SAMPLES
of something
known illusively
as raspberry-caramel-
chocolato

(popular only
with the very
pregnant or
very stoned)

READING FREE
MAGAZINE,
LISTENING TO
FREE MUSIC, AND
TEXT MESSAGING FOR FREE
ON FREE CELL WITH
FREE AIRTIME.

FREE NEWSPAPERS
is it OK to
take these with m

↳ inside the big city / small suburb / maxi-mall / mini-mall /
coffeeshop / bookstore

BOOKS 'N' STUFF

POSSIBLY HOMELESS,
POSSIBLY VERY HIP
BARISTA

FREE BITS
of some sort of
breakfast cookie
that makes you cough

FREE BACKGROUND
MUSIC
But now that
I listen closely,
it seems to be
Hare krishna
folk-fusion music
to keep people
from lingering too
long

well,
then, why
am i so
poor?

LIES and HALF-TRUTHS the INTERNET TOLD ME

you are preauthorized

your e-pinion matters

it's a long-life battery

it's lightweight

it's easy

it's safe

it's free

it's blonde

it's exotic

it's edible

it's small

it's big

find the answer here

BIG QUESTIONS FOR "THEM"

WHY DOES EVERYTHING EXHAUST ME?

DO I DESERVE BETTER?

HAS THE ADDITION OF CHEESE SEVERED
THE CROISSANT'S CONNECTION TO FRANCE

WILL TRUCKS GET SMALL AGAIN?

IS THAT A YOUNG HOMELESS MAN OR
A SUPERMODEL?

IS WEARING A JESTER HAT OK AS LONG
AS ITS JUST FOR SNOWBOARDING?

WILL THE TAX COLLECTOR FIND ME?

WILL GLOBAL WARMING INCREASE OR
DECREASE THE NUDIST POPULATION?

That GORE-TEX guitar cozy may be
taking away (slightly) from your punk look.
And actually those mini-CD earrings are
not really working out for you either...

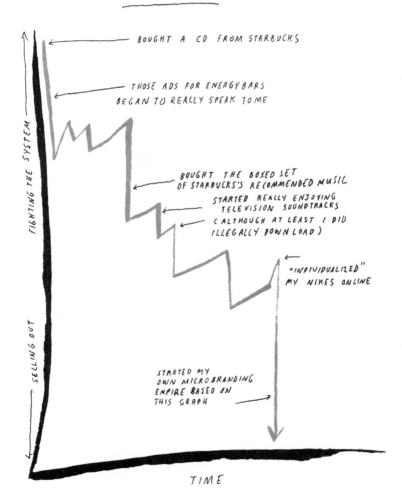

there must be SOMEONE to blame

the internet
may be at fault

?

the internet is
probably not at fault

MY GAMBLING
PROBLEM

THE FACT THAT MY
BOYFRIEND IS SPENDING
MORE MONEY ON
FACE CREAMS THAN I AM

CHILDREN
DRINKING
LATTES

FUSION COOKING

LINDSAY LOHAN

THE END OF THE
FISHING INDUSTRY

THE DIDGERIDOO

WORLD BEAT MUSIC

THE FALSE PROMISES
OF WHITE CHOCOLATE

RISING COSTS AT
FLEA MARKETS

www.com

yep, someone
does own it.

Everything you think is true.

—Prince

WHAT the KIDZ R UP 2

(some types that will never die)

 The guy who can roll joints really well

 The mean girl who everyone other than you seems to think is really nice

 The guy with orange hair who drinks a lot of orange pop

 The guy who really knows how to work a sweater vest

(and some new types)

The druid
the party planner
the exclusive reclusive
the un-nervous nerd
the idiot-cum-know-it-all

I blog you

I blog you, too

THE NEW INFORMATION ECONOMY

Connecting you with the ex that you thought you had left behind in that small town and whose name you had just about permanently erased from your memory

8 PM , WEDNESDAY

IT'S OUT THERE ON THE LINE

YOU DO THE MATH

SERVER DOWN

\+

ANTI-DEPRESSANTS

\+

PRIDE WEEKEND

\+

WELFARE CHEQUE

\+

BLUE HAIR

\+

BROKEN HEART

\=

2 LARGE A
PROBLEM
2 FIX

REALITY BYTES

summertime , but my feeling is uneasy

your Barista
Recommends

caramel-free
double
Zen soy
chillatte

AND also RECOMMENDS

that you give up your
attempts to woo her
with that miniature
Eiffel Tower you have
sculpted out of
coffee-cup sleeves...

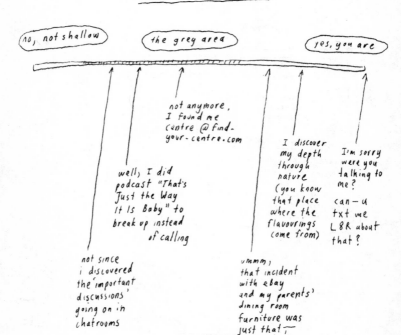

folders
can
help

ORGANIZE YOUR WORRIES

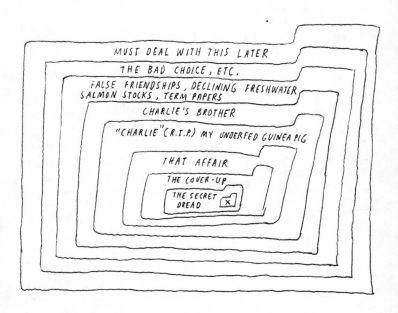

MUST DEAL WITH THIS LATER

THE BAD CHOICE, ETC.

FALSE FRIENDSHIPS, DECLINING FRESHWATER
SALMON STOCKS, TERM PAPERS

CHARLIE'S BROTHER

"CHARLIE" (R.I.P.) MY UNDERFED GUINEA PIG

THAT AFFAIR

THE COVER-UP

THE SECRET
DREAD

HAVE YOU STILL GOT IT?

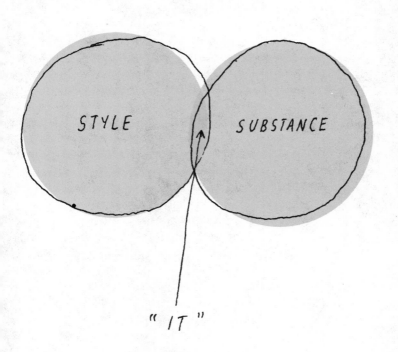

"IT"

DAVE

PROBABLY   NEVER   WILL

"GET WITH"

A SUPERMODEL

DIRTY or FUTURISTIC — you make the call

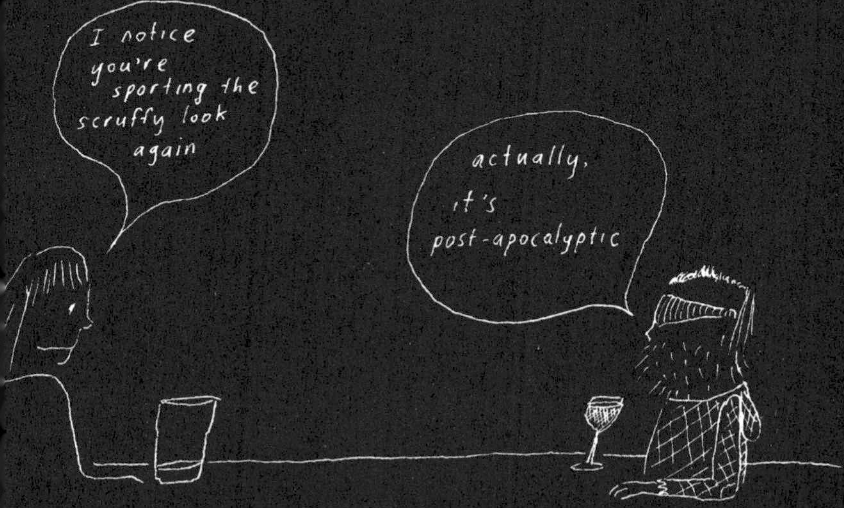

REALITY CHECK

Can you

MATCH YOUR VIRTUAL
"Dream Date"
TO THE REAL THING?

I'VE BEEN TOLD I'M QUITE GOOD LOOKING

WHY YES, I DO HAVE MY OWN TRUCK

LET'S JUST SAY I HAVE A SURFER'S BODY

I'M NOT WEARING ANYTHING!

The answer lies somewhere in the middle

BEFORE YOU MEET YOUR PerfectMatch INTERNET
DATE, YOU MIGHT WANT TO COME CLEAN
ABOUT A FEW THINGS...

(Let's start a checklist)

☐ WASH FACE

☐ ADMIT THAT YOU MAY HAVE EXAGGERATED
  YOUR SIZE BY A FEW PIXELS

☐ ALSO ADMIT THE PHOTOSHOP WORK
  THAT YOU'VE HAD DONE

☐ RECONSIDER YOUR WHITE SPORT SOCKS
  WITH DRESS SHOES LOOK

☐ CLEAR UP THE FACT THAT THE
  WAY YOU "TALK" ON THE WEB
  IS BASED ON Thesaurus.com,
  WHILE THE WAY YOU TALK IN
  PERSON IS SORT of BASED ON
  CAVEMEN and THE SIMPSONS

GETTING LOADED

welcome to
drunk emailing

→ R U AS DRUNK AS ME ?

↳ I'm NOT SURE, WHO R U ?

IS HE "ALL THAT":
let's take a look at the evidence

- [ ] A girlfriend for each name he is going by these days

- [ ] I believe that moustache is a fake

- [ ] He did make me dinner one night (over the internet)

- [ ] The memories (such as they are) HAVE mostly been captured on digital video

- [ ] And he claims that the incident in the hot tub involved me too, although the footage is too grainy to tell

- [ ] He probably WOULD settle down if he weren't being evicted

- [ ] And I suppose he did customize that e-valentine

- [ ] Plus, his friendsters seem like decent people

- [ ] OK, you're right, he's all chat

HOW TO MAKE WHAT IS CLEARLY JUST AN ONLINE FLING SEEM LIKE AN AUTHENTIC ROMANCE

① keep the lights dimmed
② pour some wine (quite a bit)
③ put on a little music
④ and maybe just keep your eyes closed while you're at it

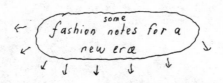

some fashion notes for a new era

DIGITAL DEVICES

There's something about a little green blinking light that goes with almost any outfit (except for maybe this one)

THE NEW BLACK

actually black has gone back to just being black again

BILLOWY PANTS

I noticed them on the kids of Paris but maybe its old now

worn with chinese slippers, I believe

SPACE-AGE FABRICS?

check out these pants

any fabric calling itself "space age" is probably verging on being retro by now

CONDOS

pretty much anything you can squeeze a bed and a hot plate into is a condo

POINTY SHOES

pointy shoes will just keep getting pointier until (frankly) they become a health risk

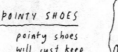

why SHOULD I BOTHER TO REINVENT myself?

ONE QUESTION, MANY ANSWERS

- [ ] BECAUSE EVERYONE ELSE IS DOING IT

- [ ] BECAUSE TUBE-SOCKS WITH SANDALS IS ONLY THE GATEWAY TO YOUR PROBLEMS

- [ ] BECAUSE MOST PEOPLE HAVE EITHER LOST, OR NEVER REALLY HAD, A "GROOVE"

- [ ] BECAUSE YOU CAN

- [ ] BECAUSE MYSPACE IS YOUR SPACE

- [ ] BECAUSE GARAGE ROCK HAS PRETTY MUCH PLAYED ITSELF OUT

- [ ] BECAUSE SMOKING A PIPE JUST LOOKS SO DISTINGUISHED

- [ ] BECAUSE EVERYONE IS WATCHING

- [ ] BECAUSE SALON - BEAUTIFUL HAIR IS POSSIBLE

POWERS of 10 (number crunching)

10^1 ————————————→ AS CLOSE AS I CAN GET TO SLEEPING WITH YOU (IN BLOCKS)

10^{10} ————————————→ NUMBER OF DAYS IT TAKES TO GROW A BEARD

10^{100} ————————————→ NUMBER OF HAIRS IN THAT BEARD

10^{1000} ————————————→ NUMBER OF TIMES I'VE LOOKED IN THE MIRROR

$10^{10,000}$ ————————————→ NUMBER OF LETTERS I'LL NEITHER WRITE NOR SEND

$10^{100,000}$ ————————————→ WHY DIDN'T SHE LIKE THE BEARD?

————→ HEY, BY THE WAY, HOW MUCH IS A GOOGLE?

$10^{100,000,000}$ ————————————→ WHY WASN'T THE BEARD ENOUGH TO MAKE HER LOVE ME?

$10^{100,000,000,000}$ ————————————→ MAYBE I SHOULD JUST SHAVE IT OFF — IT LOOKS STUPID ANYWAY

$10^{100,000,000,000,000}$ ————————————→ OH, I'M SORRY, WERE WE TALKING ABOUT MATH?

It's true that
the man of
your dreams
is somewhere
out there on
the net—
but then again
so is the man
of your nightmares.

<u>REPEAT</u>

WHY CAN'T I
USE THIS

 AUTO REVERSE

function

FOR EVERYTHING

IN

MY LIFE ?

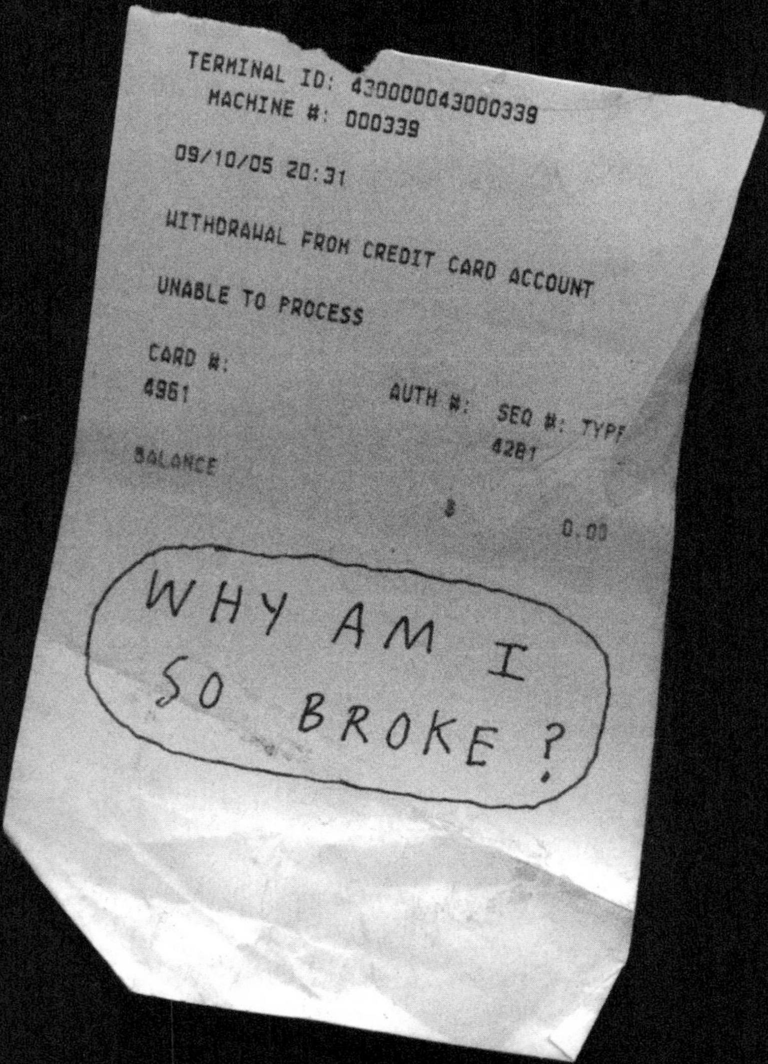
TERMINAL ID: 430000043000339
MACHINE #: 000339
09/10/05 20:31
WITHDRAWAL FROM CREDIT CARD ACCOUNT
UNABLE TO PROCESS
CARD #:
4961
AUTH #:
SEQ #: TYPE
4281
BALANCE
$
0.00
WHY AM I SO BROKE?

When you're far from home, you start living in your music. Music is my true home!

—Brian Eno

ST. ALBERT PUBLIC LIBRARY
5 ST. ANNE STREET
ST. ALBERT, ALBERTA T8N 3Z9

HOW SECURE IS YOUR CONNECTION?

I JUST SENT MY CREDIT CARD INFORMATION TO THE SAVE THE AFRICAN PENGUINS RELIEF FUND, SHOULD I BE WORRIED?

WELL, I WAS WONDERING IF IT'S A COINCIDENCE THAT SOMEONE WITH MY NAME AND ADDRESS SEEMS TO BE SELLING SOMETHING CALLED "THE SILK-WORM CURE" ONLINE.

I'M STILL WAITING IN LINE AT THE BANK.

SECRET SAFETY DEPOSIT BOX, UNDERGROUND BUNKER, ZURICH : ANY OTHER QUESTIONS?

plan for later

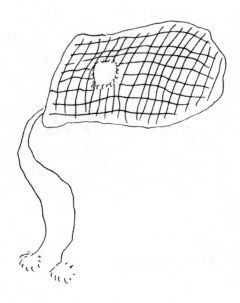

CROCHET YOUR OWN iPod COZY

Fun! Free! Stuff!

people watching
cigarette butt reclamation
simple hand puppets
those crackers you get with soup
the internet at school,
but somehow it doesn't
feel like fun to me

ADD IT UP

where the money goes

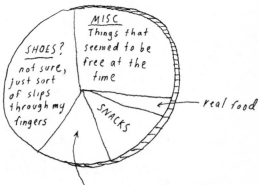

MISC
Things that seemed to be free at the time

SHOES?
not sure, just sort of slips through my fingers

SNACKS

real food

where it comes from

OK, most of it IS from my parents. But getting fired from Kinko's was not entirely my fault

AUTOMATIC PAYMENTS
can't remember what I signed up for but this section seems to be related to a birding hobbie that someone with the same name as me has

WHAT'S LEFT OF THE OLD STUDENT LOAN

The quick-purchase problem

DESPITE THE <u>MANY</u> ADVANCES
IN MODERN TEXTILE MANUFACTURING
RESEARCH, YOU MIGHT WANT TO
RECONSIDER YOUR RECENT ONLINE
PURCHASE OF UNBLEACHED ORGANIC
HEMP RUSK BRIEFS.

now that you've graduated

YOU MAY HAVE TIME TO DO

A FEW OF THE FOLLOWING

- [ ] REDUCE DEGREE AND PUT ON KEYCHAIN
- [ ] DO SOME HALF-HEARTED SEARCHING ON MONSTER.COM
- [ ] GO FREELANCE
- [ ] DEVELOP SOME "IMPORTANT THEORIES"
- [ ] DOWNLOAD THE FULL LYRICS TO THAT TOM PETTY SONG ABOUT LIVING LIKE A REFUGEE
- [ ] GET SOME OF THAT HIP HOP MONEY
- [ ] GET SHIT TOGETHER, PUBLISH IT ON LIVEJOURNAL

WHO IN THE
HELL IS CRAIG
AND HOW COME
HE KNOWS SO MANY
OF THE PEOPLE WHO
ARE SUBLETTING
MY APARTMENT?

I MUST NOT (SUBMIT)

ALL THAT GLITTERS...

All that glitters is not gold and something purchased for $495 on a site called eBAYA is probably not the "one ring to rule them all",

OR JUST RESTING UP FOR
WHEN EVERYTHING CHANGES ...

Over the counter

PIECE
of the
PIE
——
$ 7

PIECE
of the
PUZZLE
$ 122

BROKE?

maybe those entrepreneurial
       kids milling about in the
suburbs have some ideas for us...

EVERYTHING
IS
WORK

The final
key to the way
I promote is
bravado. I play
to people's
fantasies.

—Donald Trump

Did you download your PhD?

IT'S OKAY, ALL OF THE FOLLOWING RESPONSES WILL HELP YOU SOUND BOOK SMART and PRETTY WELL STOP THE ACADEMIC TALK IN ITS TRACKS

downloadable

ESSAY IDEAS (PERHAPS BETTER LEFT UNDOWNLOADED)

→ STRUDEL MISCONSTRUED : A German Study

→ 4325 WAYS TO SIMPLIFY YOUR INSANE LIFE (IN POINT FORM)

→ GOOGLE V. GOGAL : New Russian Theory

→ CUNEIFORM EMOTICONS : The overlooked connection

→ e-Valentines : A MODERN FOLKLORIC PAPER

→ APPLE CRISP : Problems in American Culture

→ HOT WATER BOTTLES VS. HOT AIR BALLOONS A Study in Overinflation

→ Is Dancing the Fifth Dimension ? A PSUEDO-SCIENTIFIC INQUIRY

→ IS LANGUAGE LANGUISHING ? An Information Studies Thesis

→ "What happened in Vegas did not (Alas) stay in Vegas" : AN INDEPTH STUDY

LOOKING FOR WORK?

before you go to that job interview you might
want to:

1) TRACK DOWN AN UNWRINKLED OUTFIT

2) DOUBLE-CHECK MEDIABISTRO.COM

3) REPLACE THE LEOPARD-PRINT WALLPAPER
   ON YOUR WEBSITE

4) ALSO GET RID OF "I DON'T WANT TO
   WORK (JUST WANT TO BANG ON ME
   DRUM ALL DAY)" THEME SONG FROM
   YOUR BLOG

5) ACTUALLY, GETTING A CLOSER LOOK
   AT IT, YOU MIGHT WANT TO REMOVE
   YOUR BLOG PERMANENTLY FROM THE
   PUBLIC SPHERE

THE HONEST CV

2003 - present

while I used to seem like an "edgy" node of the youth culture, I'm now mostly just an out-of-work junior advertising copywriter with a coke problem.

Please hire me.

(Living at home)

CALL 398 4444

NEW JOBS that seem to be a bit of a
flash in the pan, but then again, who knows?

▷ SUBWAY TAI CHI INSTRUCTOR

▷ INTERNET PET CUSTODY LAWYER

▷ ROADIE FOR "THE MEXICAN ANSWER TO
   DEPECHE MODE"

▷ WEB DESIGNER FOR CARAMELJUICYBLING.COM

▷ MAXIMALIST PAINTER

▷ NANO-CARPENTER

▷ ASSISTANT TO THE WOMAN WHO MAKES
   ALL THE LISTS

▷ RANDOM NUMBER GENERATOR

MASH UPS

monster.com + Google map =
locate sites for potential jobs
   + IceRocket blog search =
locate future boss's favourite place
to drink in those areas

+ secret webcam =
   watch boss order drink
   + Flikr = pictures of this whole scene
   + your own brain and ingenuity =

congratulations, you have a job
interview for the assistant to the
JUNIOR BARISTA position.

hey, freelancers

IT'S PRETTY MUCH ALWAYS
CASUAL FRIDAY AT THE (MY)
HOME OFFICE

THE OFFICE-SPEAK DECODER

...THAT IS, IF YOU SHOULD EVER BE FORCED TO WORK

"Let's be realistic"	"let's speak in aphorisms"
"she is no longer associated with the company"	"I fired her"
office casual	the way you look when you really clean yourself up
"It's an opportunity to learn"	you will not be paid. Nor, for that matter, will you learn all that much
We are ethnically diverse	"Just so long as you look like one of those people from the American Apparel ads"

THE WEBMASTER'S BATHROBE

(AS A MATTER OF FACT, HE IS
               NAKED RIGHT NOW)

TO: [ALL EMPLOYEES]
RE: [DO YOU HAVE THE WANDERING URGE?]

MESSAGE: INDEED, WE HERE AT GLOBALWORLDCORP ARE NOMADIC BY NATURE. AND FOR THAT VERY REASON I HAVE REQUESTED WHEELS FOR <u>MANY</u> OF YOUR OFFICE CHAIRS.

AND I MIGHT ALSO NOTE <u>SOMEONE</u> HAS (IN A MOMENT OF DEVIL-MAY-CARE TOMFOOLERY) ADDED A JAUNTY SOMBRERO TO THE WATER COOLER :) YOUR BOSS

ATTACHMENT

for some reason I pictured a little more natural light up here
THE TOP

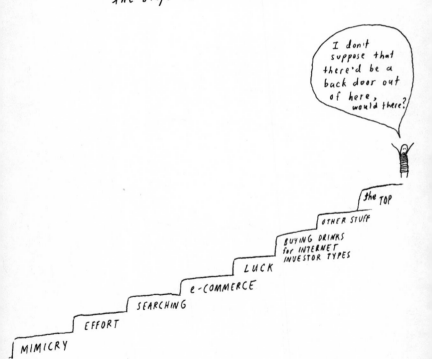

SAY, WHAT IF NEW TECHNOLOGY IS ACTUALLY DRIVEN BY OLD PEOPLE WHO ONLY CALL IT A YOUTH MOVEMENT SO THAT THEY CAN FEEL YOUTHFUL AGAIN?

class="red_hover"

relationship with Nick,

personally and professionally,
4. th

Posted in Fred Seibert's B

<a href media/470" target=_new>

class="red_hover">Diane and D

season4.php" target="_blank" cla

.frederator.com

" target="_

checked out the <a

and permission to post

s.frederator.com/post/3

href="http://newtoons

Check Your

newtoons.frederator

o<br

idea to pitch, do

<a href= toon/455" targ

t/246" target=_blank" class=

Shorts, People <b

Self-Inflicted

New Toons, New Toons, New To

Sh br/>Stay ooned

Too A Fis o's Who To

Do Toons <br/> kie Walkie

oeia

D

Frying animation

Kaz

Shorts... Stop!

Toons

Needs New Shorts!
H

Desire

Short and sweee!
Twist and Sh

2D Fruity

class="red_hover">Aliki Theofilopo

Backatcha! Cartoo

Town
 Toon Beat <b> Cartoons Th

oons Right Here!

O-R ma
Fly M The Too

n/yaki_and_yumi"

Candy Whoopee

Cartoon Street

 Do town Cartoo

WooHoo Cartoons!

Cartoon Punch

The Funny!
Cartoo

y Cartoon Space</f>

Brain Beeder
Cartoo

Cartoon Blog

Bites
Cartoon Punch <

YAY! Its a Cartoon'

Crackin Cartoons

ation Kingdom
Jumbo Laugh

Toon!
Cave Dr

WHAT'S NEW?

And what is
actual is actual
for one time
and only for
one place.

—T.S. Eliot

OUTER SPACE

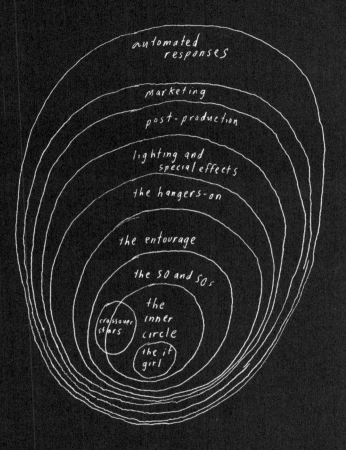

automated responses

marketing

post-production

lighting and special effects

the hangers-on

the entourage

the SO and SOs

crossover stars

the inner circle

the it girl

where I seem to be these days

HOW TO

BECOME COOL

▷ don't talk to the experts, they will only rob you of your finesse

▷ Have a close look at cucumbers

▷ make subtle references to an elusive past i.e. "...but that was...back when I was...a butter sculptor"

STAY COOL

▷ stay away from clusters

▷ watch the alleys for people who could steal your mojo

▷ go into a period of dormancy?

▷ stop using that word mojo

LEAVE THE WHOLE CONCEPT OF COOL BEHIND

▷ are you sure this is not just some other less obvious form of being cool?

ON TARGET or WAY OFF THE MARK?

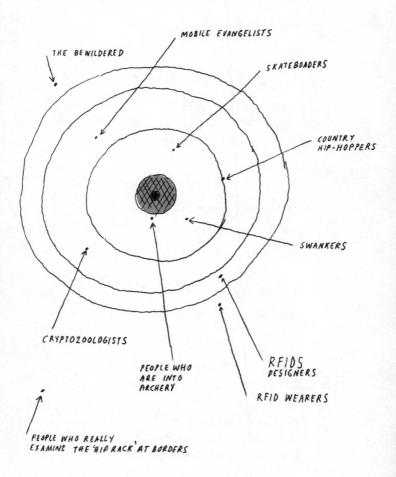

THE BEWILDERED

MOBILE EVANGELISTS

SKATEBOARDERS

COUNTRY HIP-HOPPERS

SWANKERS

CRYPTOZOOLOGISTS

PEOPLE WHO ARE INTO ARCHERY

RFIDS DESIGNERS

RFID WEARERS

PEOPLE WHO REALLY EXAMINE THE 'HIP RACK' AT BORDERS

THE NEW Elite

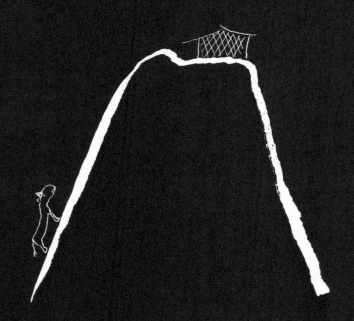

EVEN IDIOTS ARE DRIVING BENTLEYS.

＊

AIR TRAVEL IS JUST GETTING MORE AND MORE ACCESSIBLE

＊

YOU CAN FIND OUT WHAT THE BLUE BLOODS ARE EATING,
DRINKING AND TALKING ABOUT IN 2 SECONDS ONLINE

＊

PERHAPS TRUE LUXURY IS TO BE FOUND HIGH ATOP THE
MOUNTAIN IN A LITTLE SHACK ISOLATED FROM ALL
BUT THE MOST ADVENTURESOME OF MOUNTAIN GOATS.
(OR IS THAT, IN FACT, A BABY UNICORN?)

STRANGE)))))),,,,,
FREQUENCIES
a survey of the airwaves

27 MHz	TOP 10 countdowns which all seem to be East Indian versions of early Madonna
57 MHz	The Podcasts of losers
58-82	Canadian divas
33.1 MHz	Secret messages that only your budgie can pick up
127 MHz	politically correct
128	politically incorrect
132.1	let's just leave this open for the aliens
154.8	responsible for that delicious microwaved popcorn taste

stuck in

THE MATRIX

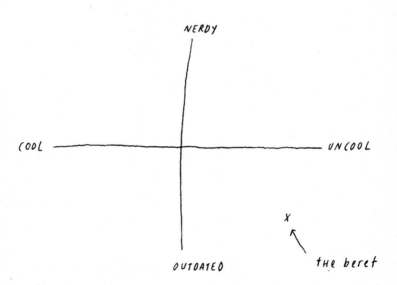

NERDY

COOL ———————————— UNCOOL

OUTDATED

X
↑
the beret

2 PM, a field

KIND OF BEAUTIFUL,
KIND OF SPREADING
UNCONTROLLABLY

try to stay cool WITH ORIGAMI

first fold
HIGH-TECH AMERICA GOES RETRO 80s

second fold
BUT IN THE 80s EVERYONE IN AMERICA WAS REFERENCING THE JAPANESE

third fold
OK, BUT AT THE TIME THE JAPANESE WERE IMAGINING A FUTURE AMERICA SURROUNDED BY TECHNOLOGY

fourth fold
STILL, IF THEY HAD IMAGINED RIGHT THEY WOULD HAVE SEEN THAT HIGH-TECH WOULD LOOP BACK ON ITSELF

fifth fold
OK. ALL FINISHED. NOW, YOU TELL ME, DOES IT LOOK MORE LIKE A ROBOT OR A CRANE?

COULD GRECO-ROMAN CULTURE HELP US OUT?

how's about we put the current situation in the context of ancient myths

ALL FLASH

SORT OF CUTE,
SORT OF JAPANESE
AND, BLESS ITS LITTLE HEART,
SORT OF SEEMS TO BE
TRYING TO SELL YOU AN
UPGRADE

BUT HOW WILL THE VAMPIRES BE AFFECTED BY THE NEW TECHNOLOGY?

a bat
not sure how he fits in

TRANSYLVANIAN CASTLE
I believe they're
making software
knockoffs here now

MORNING the natural
enemy of the
vampire and
a few other people
I know

Trust me, there's
plenty of
downloadable options
for vampire music

(and those earbuds
are pretty inconspicuous)

iPod "skin" sounds kind
of vampire-like

velvet seems to be giving
way to velour among the
goths

HELL, NO ONE'S
feeling all that
alive these days

FAKE BLOOD? REAL BLOOD?
I'm sure its all for sale on
the net somewhere

victorianfancyboots.uk.org

SPENDING MOST
OF YOUR DAY IN
A DARK CAVE IS
PRACTICALLY A
LINCHPIN OF THE
NEW ECONOMY

THE NON-STOP TRAVELLER

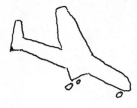

YOU NEVER REALLY TOUCHED DOWN

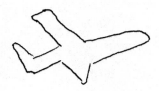

BUT THEN, YOU NEVER REALLY TOOK OFF EITHER

NAVIGATING THE SCENE

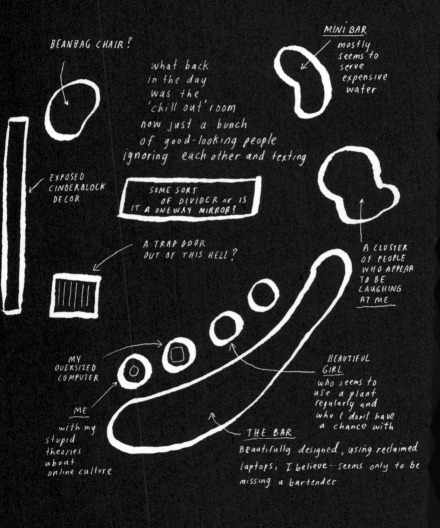

BEANBAG CHAIR?

MINI BAR
mostly
seems to
serve
expensive
water

what back
in the day
was the
'chill out' room
now just a bunch
of good-looking people
ignoring each other and texting

EXPOSED
CINDERBLOCK
DECOR

SOME SORT
OF DIVIDER or IS
IT A ONE WAY MIRROR?

A TRAP DOOR
OUT OF THIS HELL?

A CLUSTER
OF PEOPLE
WHO APPEAR
TO BE
LAUGHING
AT ME

MY
OVERSIZED
COMPUTER

BEAUTIFUL
GIRL
who seems to
use a plant
regularly and
who I don't have
a chance with

ME
with my
stupid
theories
about
online culture

THE BAR
Beautifully designed, using reclaimed
laptops, I believe - seems only to be
missing a bartender

A MESSAGE

ACTUALLY THOSE
LITTLE GAMES
ON YOUR CELL
WERE DESIGNED
TO ACTIVATE THE
BOREDOM...

Dearest Europeans

I'm writing you this letter because I can't seem to get my email over here.

While I _have_ learned to pronounce the word "grande" (that is your language, isn't it?) and I _do_ respect that you are unionized — and _furthermore_ I realize that without your castles we wouldn't have had a clue about how to start building Disneyland and _also_ without your SPAGHETTI BOLOGNESE I personally would be a lesser person —

Still why must you pronounce Wifi like Wee Fee as if it is some sort of poodle (which by the way I believe that you invented)? And why don't you have it free _in_ all of your café's like we do?

Chiao!

a tourist

WHAT IS ON THE CUTTING EDGE

(and will it hurt)?

PILGRIM Costumes
FLUORESCENT ALGAE
parts of HELSINKI
most of BERLIN
RUNNING SHOES WITH A SPLIT TOE
the ANTARCTIC UNDERGROUND
DARK NETS
MEMES
BLOGJECTS
VERTICAL FARMING
RETRO TECHNO
REVERSE ENGINEERING
DIY

(and is that some kind of
sushi knife you've drawn there?)

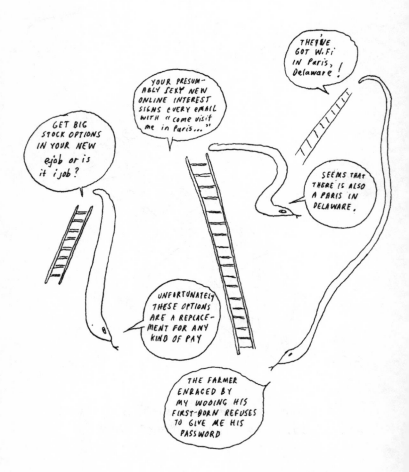

WHAT THEY'RE THINKING ABOUT IN...*

MESOPOTAMIA .... birding

LONDON .... <u>Footloose: the musical</u>

TRANSYLVANIA .... software knock-offs mostly

AMERICA .... dietcoke + mentos + suburban
                             parking lots = tons o' fun

SCANDINAVIA .... ducttape which they call "jesus tape"

ALAPAHA, GEORGIA .... Hogzilla, the 800 lb boar

ARGENTINA .... wine bandits

JAPAN .... the effect of Tsunamis on mushrooms

BARCELONA .... all night parties, tinnitus

PARIS .... sports generally, sailboat racing in particular

FINLAND .... Eurovision, 1969

THE ALTERNET .... Barrak Obama

* THAT IS, ACCORDING TO MY TOTALLY ARBITRARY RESEARCH

WELCOME TO THE FUTURE

You can't
connect the dots
looking forward;
you can only
connect them
looking
backwards.

—Steve Jobs

ALL THE
STUFF
THAT IS
GOING ON
OUT THERE

AND YET I FEEL
STUCK INSIDE
MYSELF...

The maze you're stuck in today

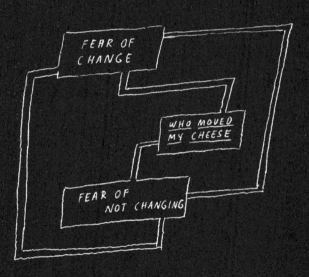

A FLOW CHART I NEVER REALLY GOT AROUND TO FINISHING

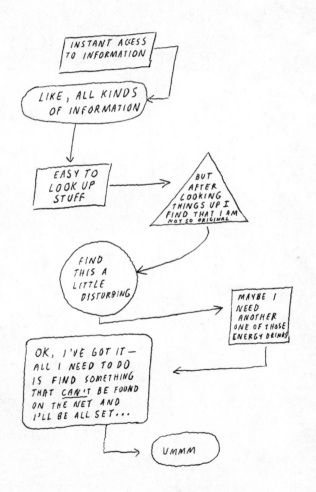

EVERYTHING IS IN FLUX

let's have a look at the four elements
what's going on

sort of COOL

THINGS I FOUND OUT ABOUT ON THE NET TODAY

↳ CAB CALLOWAY COINED THE PHRASE
"ROCK and ROLL"

↳ THERE IS A BAR IN EAST BERLIN
THAT FRISKS PEOPLE FOR CELLPHONES
AND CAMERAS INSTEAD OF DRUGS AND GUNS

↳ SOMEONE HAS MARKETED A BED THAT
FLOATS ON THE CEILING WHEN IT'S NOT
BEING USED

↳ NORMAL CDs HAVE A SHORT SHELF LIFE

↳ SOMEONE HAS WRITTEN A BOOK ABOUT
PUNK FENG SHUI

↳ CANDLES ARE A $200-BILLION-A-YEAR
BUSINESS

↳ I THINK I AM ABOUT TO CRASH

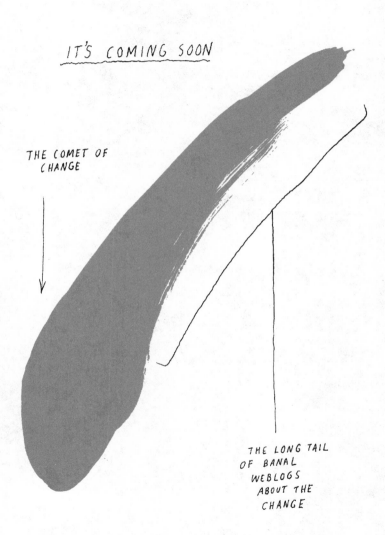

IT'S COMING SOON

THE COMET OF
CHANGE

THE LONG TAIL
OF BANAL
WEBLOGS
ABOUT THE
CHANGE

Sometimes it seems that
we <u>are</u> living in the space age

HAVE A CLOSE LOOK

0101010101010101010101010101010101010101010
1010101010101010101010101010101010101010101
0101010101010101010101010101010101010101010
1010101010101010101010101010101010101010101
1010101010101 THE 0101010101010101010101010
0101010101010101010101010101010101010101010
1010101010101010101010101010101010101010101
0101010101010101010101 TECHNOLOGY 101010
1010101010101010101010101010101010101010101
0101010101010101010101010101010101010101010
1010101010101010101010101010101010101010101
0101010101010101010101010101010101010101010
101010 HAS 0101010101010101010101010101010
0101010101010101010101 NO 1010101010101010
1010101010101010101010101010101010101010101
0101010101010101010101010101010101010101010
1010101010101010101010101010101010101010101
0101010101010101010101010101010101010101010
0101010 MORAL 0101010101010101010101010101
1010101010101010101010101010101010101010101
0101010101010101010101010101010101010101010
0101010101010101010101010101010101010101010
01010101010101010101010101010 CODE 1010101010
1010101010101010101010101010101010101010101

<s>the</s> ALIENS TRY TO DESCRIBE
THE WAY WE LIVE

⟨ FIG A ⟩   FETISH OBJECTS:

① circular, flat disk that when placed inside magic box will cause fire patterns that will excite the participant

③

② small, flat rounded tablet enscribed with circular disk will bring forth sounds of the goddess known as "Britney," initiating repetitive self-praising and joined in this ritual by the animal god known as Snoop Dogg

mysterious clam-shaped object that seems to call forth to similar clam-shaped objects which, when in unison, create an invisible sacred space known as "myspace"

WILL BE GARBAGE BEFORE YOU KNOW IT

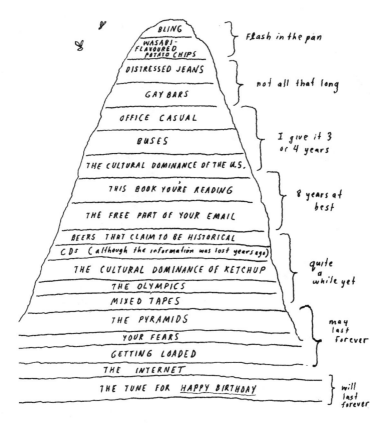

ARE YOU

sporting a new but worn-out-looking Iron Maiden T-shirt?

sporting an actually old, actually worn-out Iron Maiden T-shirt that cost you 80 bucks?

not wearing, but own a 1981 original Iron Maiden T-shirt that you have shrinkwrapped and had authenticated by an independant 3rd party?

keeping an actual iron maiden tucked away in your basement?

sporting an "Ironic Maiden" T-shirt?

CAN SOMEONE EXPLAIN THIS TO ME?

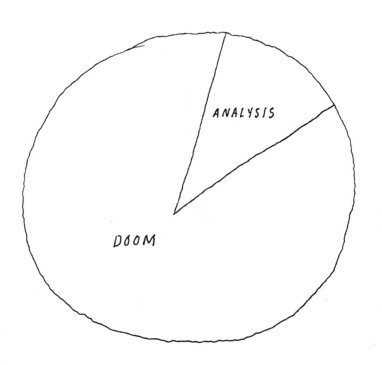

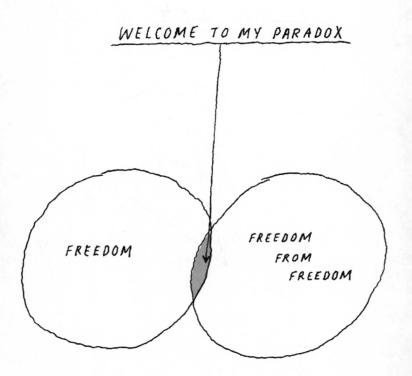

SO LAST YEAR

spelling bees
chai
snarkblogs
Johnny Cash
memoirs
chillattes
lower back tattoo removal
cool hunting
the Kabbalah
lists

NEXT YEAR

the glaciers!

BY THE TIME YOU READ THIS...

→ there will be bottled water tasting bars

→ there will be some very fancy underwear for men

→ the word stocastic will mean something to you

→ there won't be any outsider artists left

→ unbranding will have lost all its cachet

→ the only real scenes will be in the suburbs

→ your parents will be explaining the internet to you

→ malt flavouring will take over from where caramel left off

Hey Californians

WOULD YOU PLEASE STOP INVENTING
THINGS THAT MAKE ME FEEL LIKE MY
FINGERS ARE GIGANTIC SAUSAGES

Plus WHAT'S UP WITH
THE OC ?

NIGHT and DAY

my Projects

TO DO TODAY

- ☐ GET LOADED
- ☐ JOIN ONLINE FIGHT AGAINST THE HORDES OF THE UNDEAD
- ☐ GO TO WORK

TO DO IN SOME YET-TO-BE-REALIZED FUTURE

- ☐ COME TO TERMS WITH THE INFORMATION AGE
- ☐ ATTEND GARLIC FESTIVAL
- ☐ REWORK MY MEMOIRS (WITH LINKS)
- ☐ STOP GOOGLING MYSELF
- ☐ TRY TO CURB MY APPETITE FOR THESE MEANINGLESS BOXES
- ☐ START WEARING SUNSCREEN
- ☐ HAVE A CLOSER LOOK AT LABEL OF SUNSCREEN TO FIND OUT WHAT THE HELL THEY PUT IN IT

THE GREAT DIVIDE

MORE ABILITY TO BE REACHED	LESS YOU WANT TO BE REACHED
MORE CONNECTION	MORE LIKELY TO WANT TO BE ALONE
MORE OPTIONS	LESS CHOICES
MAKE MORE MONEY ON THE SELF-HELP MARKET	LESS HELPFUL
MORE ANTI-CONSUMER	MORE YOU ARE MARKETED TO
MORE KNOWLEDGE	LESS CERTAINTY
MORE CHAT	LESS CONVERSATION
MORE PEOPLE	LESS THEY UNDERSTAND YOU
MORE SECURITY MEASURES	LESS SECURE YOU FEEL
MORE THEY USE THE WORD SEXY	LESS SEXY IT SEEMS
MORE YOU THINK ABOUT IT	LESS IT MAKES SEN.
MORE VERSIONS	LESS MONEY TO UPGR.
MORE POWER	LESS ENERGY
MORE JOBS	LESS FUTURE
MORE FREE	LESS FREEDOM

FORTUNES!

THERE IS NO NEW BLACK.

THERE WILL ALWAYS BE SOMETHING
KIND OF COOL ABOUT DUCT TAPE.

THERE WILL BE A BIG BLACKOUT.
UNSCENTED CANDLES WILL GET EXPENSIVE,
PEOPLE WILL TRY TO GROW THEIR OWN
FOOD. THEN EVERYTHING WILL GO BACK TO NORMAL.

HEY, THE CAVE BABIES
DID FINE, SO WILL WE.

WHATEVER THE HELL THAT IS.

TANTRIC JUST MEANS
REALLY SLOW.

THE REVOLUTION IS INVISIBLE.

BIB LETTUCE.

NECESSITY IS THE
MOTHER OF MORE
NECESSITY.

HAVE YOU TRIED
MICRO-PERSUASION?

NEITHER ROBOTS NOR
DOLPHINS WILL END UP
TAKING OVER FROM US.

I'M NOT SURE WHAT IS GOING
ON ONLINE, BUT IT SEEMS TO HAVE
SOMETHING TO DO WITH MAJOR CUTE GUYS.

THAT SANTA OVER THERE IS
DRUNK. SAME GOES FOR
THE CROSSING GUARD.

ASK THE FORKLIFT
OPERATOR.

EVERYTHING AROUND YOU IS
A POTENTIAL FUTURE ANTIQUE.

REACH FOR THE STARS,
FIND THAT THEIR WEBSITE IS STILL
UNDER CONSTRUCTION.

THE FUTURE LOOKS BRIGHT,
A LITTLE TOO BRIGHT IF YOU
ASK ME.

S TIME SPENDING.

R.I.P. V.I.P.

BLOGS ARE THE NEW MIRRORS.

THERE'S NO TIME LIKE
THE FUTURE.

THERE'S NOT MUCH GOING
ON IN THE INNER CIRCLE.

SEEK NOT A PLACE
IN OPRAH'S BOOK CLUB.

GET IT WHILE YOU STILL
REMEMBER WHAT "IT" IS.

START A RUMBLE!

EVERYTHING WILL BE THE SAME
IN THE FUTURE EXCEPT THAT
IT WILL HAVE ROUNDED CORNERS.

YOUR COMPUTER MAY HELP YOU
TO CULTIVATE THE FARAWAY
LOOK.

E THE MAN WITH PIGTAILS
HE WOMAN WITH THE LONG
D SKIRT.

EVERYTHING IS A FAD.

REINVENTION CAN MAKE A
PERSON SLEEPY.

WE'VE STILL GOT A FEW YEARS
TO FIGURE OUT WHAT TO DO
ABOUT THE SUN EXPLODING.

YOU WILL EAT A LOT, GO INTO A
PERIOD OF DORMANCY, AND EMERGE
AS AN ONLINE BUTTERFLY CONSULTANT.

IF IT'S HAPPENING, IT'S REAL,

DEFINITIONS

ATAVISM An evolutionary throwback or the unexpected appearance of primitive traits. Consider for a moment that people born with tails, medievalists, and fans of the TSR 80 might be on to something useful to future generations.

BOOM-BANG-A-BANG! A cult European audio drama based on the long-running British science fiction television series *Doctor Who*. The title is a parody of 1969's Eurovision Song Contest winner, Lulu's "Boom-Bang-a-Bang!" Its significance remains to be seen.

CONCEPTUAL AGE (THE) Daniel Pink's theory for *Wired* magazine that the information age is coming to an end. Everything technical or mathematical can be done better in the Third World, plus raw information is cheap. The real jobs will be in realms that technology can't touch: creativity, emotion, and intuition. In other words, a B.A. from some hippy college in the Midwest is your best bet for the future.

DISAMBIGUATION A term popularized on Wikipedia for separating out the various meanings of a single word. Sometimes an attempt to disambiguate words can lead you down a weird path. For example, "emo" can refer to a sub-genre of hardcore punk, the nickname of the wide receiver for the Houston Texans, a type of online currency, a Canadian emergency preparedness organization, an acronym in lacrosse, an Irish oil company and filling station chain, and a 16th-century villa in Italy.

E Euler's number, a transcendental number (approximately equal to 2.71828182845904523536028747135352) that is used as the base for natural logarithms. *Pi* is so last year.

FOLKSONOMY An underground system for labelling things. What started out as a bunch of kids "tagging" their bad digital photos is rapidly becoming a community-based intuitive means of connecting images and ideas on the net. Plus have you ever been to one of those folksonomy conferences? Those people know how to party.

GROK Coined in science fiction writer Robert A. Heinlein's 1961 novel *Stranger in a Strange Land.* In the Martian tongue, it translates as "to drink," but it also means to understand so thoroughly that the observer becomes a part of the observed. The term gained real-world currency as slang among counterculture groups, including hippies. Today it is chiefly used by science fiction fans, geeks, and some pagans.

HIVE MIND The idea that the collective (say, bees or internet users) may be working on a pattern that is bigger and more complex than any one of their individual understandings. In *Emergence,* Steven Johnson looks at the higher intelligence of ants, cities, the human brain, and new technology. The flip side of this idea, "coblabberation" (from Harvard professor David Perkins), suggests that a bunch of people working together without any real understanding of the whole can create a bit of a mess.

IN-GAME WEDDINGS It's true. People are getting married inside games. Particularly, huge multi-player role-playing fantasy games that include dragons and magic. The phenomenon has become big enough that 1) there are online in-game wedding planners and guides, and 2) some guy at Stanford University is studying it.

JOYBUBBLES A kind of bizarre father figure for the hackers (*see* **Phreaking**). Born Joe Engressia in 1949, Joybubbles (his legal name) is a blind ordained minister of his own "Church of Eternal Childhood," who can whistle at 2600 Hz (which allows him to make long distance calls for free), claims to be 5 years old, and is too interesting a character to sum up in just a few sentences.

KARMA WHORES Slashdot is a popular technology site that shares opinion without too much junk. It regulates its content by rating its users, who in turn rate the content. A good user rating on Slashdot and other sites is known as *karma*. Karma whores (or trolls) are a sub-culture within the Slashdot world who finds ways to abuse the system in order to test it, to make money from it, or just for the sake of art. Nerd-art, that is.

LONG TAIL Chris Anderson's concept in *Wired* magazine that describes business and economic models such as Amazon.com or Netflix.com that have found success not on the cutting edge but on the periphery. He notes that no one would have expected that new technology would actually mean getting rich off teenage ramblings.

MEME Coined in 1976 by Richard Dawkins, this term refers to a replicator of cultural information transmitted by one mind (verbally or by demonstration) to another. According to Dawkins, tunes, ideas, catch-phrases, fashion—and ways of making pots or of building arches—are all examples of memes. Plus, saying that you are transmitting memes sounds more impressive than saying that you are coming up with theories while drinking beer with your buddies.

NEUTRALITY DISPUTE Nothing on the net is neutral.

OY A YUBIZOKU (thumb tribe) A Japanese phrase for those who are skilled at using their thumbs to manipulate objects such as cellphone keys, small joysticks, and notebook computer pointers. According to David Kushner in *The Wireless Arcade,* an estimated 80 percent of people worldwide currently use wireless devices to connect to the net.

PHREAKING A slang term describing the activities of a subculture of people who study, experiment with, or exploit telephone companies. The coolest method is to whistle into the phone at a frequency that allows you free calls (*see* **Joybubbles**).

QUINCE Originating from Mesopotamia, this ugly but honest fruit makes a delicious jelly and some historians believe that it was the quince and not the apple that got Adam and Eve into trouble in the Garden of Eden.

RFID Radio Frequency Identification is an automatic identification method that relies on storing and remotely retrieving data using devices called RFID tags or transponders (kind of like the chip you got implanted into Rover). Night clubs in Barcelona and Rotterdam are now using RFIDs to identify their VIP customers, who in turn use it to pay for drinks. Ouch.

SCREAMO A musical genre that evolved from Emo; more specifically, a sub-sect of early 1990s emo (or emotional rock). Characteristic of the genre are hard-core screaming vocals and fast, harmonized guitars. Most Screamo songs use imagery and metaphors to communicate lost love or failed friendships.

TWEEDSTART The Scots have come up with a solution to the new breed of iPod-obsessed delinquent youths and this "new technology stuff": Tweed! And fly-fishing! A non-profit program (based out of a Scottish castle) costs about £30,000 a year to run and is currently looking for sponsors.

UNIX A computer operating system originally developed in the 1960s and 1970s by a group of AT&T Bell Lab employees. No, Mac and Windows are not the only options. You should look into it.

VICTORIAN INTERNET (THE) Think telegraph and pneumatic tubes. The idea is that instantaneous global communication is not a recent invention, but rather a development of the mid-19th century. The changes wrought by the telegraph outweigh the effects of the internet on modern society. The ability to communicate globally, in real-time, is a qualitative shift, while the modern internet is merely a quantitative shift.

WIKI A type of website that allows users to add, remove, or otherwise edit and change most content very quickly and easily. The first wiki, WikiWikiWeb, is named after the Wiki Wiki line of buses at Honolulu International Airport, Hawaii. "Wiki-wiki" means "fast" in Hawaiian. Does anything move fast in Hawaii? (Must look this up later.)

X A symbol worn on the hand to denote that someone is "straight edge" (i.e., punks without stimulants). It is also frequently tattooed on other parts of the body, or worn on clothing, sometimes in triplicate (XXX). Straight-edgers frequently also append Xs to their names ("Jack" would be written, XjackX). Straight edge itself is commonly abbreviated as "sxe."

YELLOW FLOOR An example of a SIP (statistically improbable phrase), the word combination "yellow floor" has been discovered by Amazon.com's mega computers. Automatically calculated from digitally stored books (it also calculates how many big words and how many words per sentence), "yellow floor" is found 6 times in May Sarton's book *Plant Dreaming Deep*. That same word combination is found in only a few other books, including Frank Herbert's 6th book in the *Dune* series.

ZOMBIE FLASH MOBS Arranged through the internet, people get together at a set time and place to dress up and act like zombies. Canada has some weird examples:

"Canadian flash mobs have taken the form of zombie mobs, in which people walk to a predetermined location in a 'zombie' style, shuffling stiffly and moaning 'braaains' at passers-by. One of the first documented zombie flash mobs took place in Toronto's Queen West area in October 2004. In July 2005, several dozen self-described 'hipster zombies' pretended to attack an unsuspecting medieval reenactment in Mount Royal Park in Montreal. In Vancouver, on August 27, 2005, a group of 200 to 300 zombies assembled in front of the downtown Vancouver Art Gallery, circled the gallery, travelling through two protests, marched through the Pacific Centre mall, and took the SkyTrain to a station near Main Street and Science World. The zombies paused there briefly, before attacking a few buses and then walking up Main Street 30 blocks to the cemetery. The walk down Main Street was made quite a bit easier by a spontaneous police escort, which shut down one lane of southbound traffic. This zombie sub-genre of the phenomenon has spread to the U.S., including a recent incident at the Austin, Texas, tryouts for *American Idol*." (Source: Wikipedia)

WEBLINKS

Cd lifespan:
www.informationweek.com/story/showArticle.jhtml?articleID=15800263&pgno=1

Tweedstart:
www.telegraph.co.uk/news/main.jhtml?xml=/news/2005/08/22/nfish22.
xml&sSheet=/news/2005/08/22/ixhome.html

Non-instrument navigation:
www.pbs.org/wayfinders/wayfinding.html

Joybubbles:
www.pitt.edu/~fail/joybubbles.html

Cab Calloway, original rapper:
www.popmatters.com/music/columns/ellis/051118.shtml

How to live without a job:
www.f4.ca/text/possumliving.htm

World Jump Day:
www.venehammerschlag.com/worldjumpday

Survival blog:
www.survivalblog.com

The bridgewater triangle:
www.bridgewaterpubliclibrary.org/historical_tidbits.htm

Smart mobs and Harold Reingold:
www.smartmobs.com

Lewis Mumford and the megamachine:
www.regent.edu/acad/schcom/rojc/mdic/mumford.html

ARPANET and the history of the internet:
www.isoc.org/internet/history/brief.shtml

Barack Obama:
obama.senate.gov

The Swenkas:
www.imdb.com/title/tt0457499

Where the measurements come from:
www.npl.co.uk

Problem gambling pioneer Fyodor Dostoevsky:
www.americangaming.org/rgq/rgq_detail.cfv?
id=276

Sell wasabi-flavoured peanuts:
qdbaoquan.en.alibaba.com/offerdetail/51435447/Sell_Wasabi_Flavour_
Coated_Peanut.html

"Mystery Robot Said to Solve Crimes, Find Mines in Chile":
news.nationalgeographic.com/news/2006/05/060522-robots.html

Buddhist economics:
www.worldtrans.org/whole/buddecon.html

Are you a human? (CAPTCHA test):
www.captcha.net

French croissant recipe:
www.ochef.com/r203.htm

Hobo signs and symbols:
www.slackaction.com/signroll.htm

Aesop's fables:
www.aesopfables.com

Aesop rock:
www.definitivejux.net/jukies/aesop_rock

The labyrinth society:
www.labyrinthsociety.org
www.dangermousesite.com/index2.html

Why right brainers will rule the world:
www.danpink.com

Early version of creating false identity:
www.museumofhoaxes.com/formosa.html

One laptop per child:
web.media.mit.edu/~nicholas

David Perkins collaboration vs. coblaboration:
www.pz.harvard.edu/PIs/DP.htm

Classic pong:
www.free-javascripts.com/games/pong.html

Cargo cult theory:
www.coolth.com/cargo.htm

How to grow giant vegetables:
www.findhorn.org

Spread the love:
spreadintheluv.com

Symphony for dot matrix printers:
www.theuser.org/dotmatrix/en/intro.html

Make origami with money:
members.cox.net/crandall11/money

Pigeons that blog:
research.techkwondo.com/blog/julian/181

Punk feng shui Josh Amatore Hughes:
www.randomhouse.com/catalog/display.pperl?isbn=9780307237620&view=excerpt

Inside your iPod:
www.chipmunk.nl/iPod

What rhymes with orange:
www.askoxford.com/asktheexperts/faq/aboutwords/orange?view=uk

Are Russian nesting dolls in fact Japanese?:
russian-crafts.com/nest/history.html#begin

THANK YOU

TRACY BORDIAN (SUPPORT)

DAVID COLLIER (CONNECTION)

ANDREA CROZIER (REALIZATION)

ROBERT CRUMB (THE WATER)

ANTONIO DELUCA (KEYS)

ADAM GILDERS (TALKS)

SEAN LEE and THE STUDENTS OF SHERIDAN (IDEAS)

NATALIE MATUTSCHOVSKY (ORANGE)

HEIDI SOPINKA (♡)

SUZANNE SOPINKA (COOKIES)

BALINT ZSAKO (FAKING IT)

and MAMA (WHO IS STILL OUT THERE)